HOUND AND HORN IN JEDFOREST

BEING SOME EXPERIENCES OF A SCOTTISH M.F.H.

BY

T. SCOTT ANDERSON
AUTHOR OF "HOLLOAS FROM THE HILLS"

ILLUSTRATIONS BY G. DENHOLM ARMOUR

Copyright © 2013 Read Books Ltd.
This book is copyright and may not be
reproduced or copied in any way without
the express permission of the publisher in writing

British Library Cataloguing-in-Publication Data
A catalogue record for this book is available from the
British Library

THE FOXHOUND

Hounds form a very large section of the dog family, as the term embraces all dogs which follow game either by sight or by scent. Of the hounds that follow quarry by scent we have the bloodhound, foxhound, harrier, beagle and basset. The bloodhound will hunt various quarry – able to hunt and track deer, boar and even human beings. The latter three hounds hunt mainly hares. The foxhound is used (unsurprisingly!) primarily for the pursuit of foxes.

A foxhound is a type of large hunting hound bred for its strong hunting instincts, great energy, and, like all scent hounds, a keen sense of smell. There are different breeds of foxhound, each often called simply *Foxhound* in their native countries: the *American Foxhound,* the *English Foxhound,* the *Dumfriesshire Foxhound,* the *Black and Tan Virginia Foxhound,* and the *Welsh Hound.* At what period the foxhound got its distinctive title in England is unclear, for as late as 1735 there is no such word in the "Sportsman's Dictionary." Breeding to type had been in progress for some time at the beginning of the nineteenth century though, and packs kept entirely for fox hunting became numerous throughout England and a few other countries. Individual dogs suitable for stud, or stallions as they are called in the case of hounds or beagles, were also eagerly sought after and the annual draft was sorted so as to preserve uniformity of size, speed and, in many cases, uniformity of colouring was sought for as far as possible.

In this way, the character and conformation which stamps out the English foxhound as a breed – was formed. Type in head, perfection in legs and feet, good shoulders and good bodies are all points where a single standard governs. The differences between various packs of foxhounds so far as appearance goes is little more than a difference of height, some masters preferring a larger hound, others a medium one, and some better suited with hounds an inch or so smaller.

Although speed and endurance may be considered the chief characteristics of the modern foxhound (having elbowed 'nose' from first or even second place), it must not be supposed that every strain is bred on the same lines or with the same object. Still, allowing to the fullest extent for the different sort of hound required to meet the needs of a different sort of hunting country, the English foxhound should in make and shape follow closely certain well defined lines.

The head should be of fair size and well balanced; good length of skull and muzzle, which should be broad with wide nostrils; the eye should have a bold, keen, determined look, and the whole head denote power. The neck should be long, clean, and muscular, quite free from dewlap, except when such is characteristic of a particular strain. The shoulders should be nicely sloped. To ensure speed, the elbows should be perfectly straight in a line with the body. The chest should be deep, ribs coming down well, giving a certain appearance of squareness. The back and loins should be very strong and disclose to the touch any amount of muscle. The legs should be straight and the bone great. These legs have to carry a heavy hound for many miles at a great pace over rough country. The feet should be round and compact with a hard, firm pad and strong nails. The stern should be thick at the root and carried well up. The coat should be short, dense and rather hard in texture.

The foxhound has always enjoyed enthusiastic, skilled, and often wealthy owners; he has not been dependent upon the whims and fancies of hobby breeders. On the contrary foxhound stud books have been carefully preserved for generations. The history of every important strain is carefully recorded. Foxhound breeders have thus for many years had an ideal opportunity, and have taken full advantage of it.

This text has been reprinted for its historical and its cultural significance – making for a practically useful, as well as intriguing read. We hope the reader enjoys this book.

TO MY DAUGHTER

CONTENTS

CHAP.		PAGE
I.	HOW THE NEWS CAME	1
II.	TAKING THEM OVER	12
III.	A MORNING'S EXERCISE	23
IV.	A MORNING'S CUBBING	35
V.	FIRST BLOOD	44
VI.	GETTING TO WORK	53
VII.	A DAY WITH THE DUKE	65
VIII.	A TERRIER TALK	76
IX.	BY INVITATION	86
X.	CUMMANSHEMENSLAIGE	95
XI.	A HOUND HAVER	107
XII.	SOME BY-DAYS	117
XIII.	A HILL DAY	127
XIV.	BLANK DAYS, ODD DAYS, AND A RECORD DAY	138
XV.	BILLY'S AMBITION	152

LIST OF ILLUSTRATIONS

A hill fox with his nose to the hills, and hounds screaming close behind him .	. Frontispiece		
" Let's have one more look at the Irish mare"	To face page		9
" Forager" with the carcase of a hen hanging from his jaws.	"	"	16
She slid the astonished horseman not ungracefully over her tail. . . .	"	"	24
He faced round at them with open jaws .	"	"	47
Old " Bedpost" scratching the affected leg .	"	"	54
Bobby bolted underneath it at the risk of being scraped off	"	"	67
" Scurry" lying curled up beside him growling savagely	"	"	83
With a twist of his quarters flung himself over with a foot and a half to spare .	"	"	89
Pat Murray sitting complacently on a dogcart cushion alongside his trap . .	"	"	102
We gazed at the huddled-up forms on the sleeping benches	"	"	108
Setting out on a fourteen-mile jog home .	"	"	122
" The tarrierh's oot close ahint 'im" . .	"	"	132
He was pushed on to his head and balanced there	"	"	148
She could not stay beside the old horse .	"	"	160

Hound and Horn in Jedforest

CHAPTER I

HOW THE NEWS CAME

"*Werry good indeed! most beautiful!! in fact, wot honour I arrives at!*"—J. J.

TWO horses in summer condition, big all over, were coming in from early morning exercise, and though they had only had a short two hours of slow walking, both were sweating, and the ridden one was slightly lathered on the neck and under the saddle.

It was rather more than midway between the hunting and the shooting seasons; that period dull and dead to the average hunting man, who, if he has no other hobby to ride, finds he is then a weariness to himself and a positive nuisance to his friends. But to the man who delights in country sights and sounds—and what true sportsman does not?—no time of the year in the country is dull or lifeless, and all seasons, far from being flat or profitless, are big with interest, and the days are often all too short for what they bring.

I had strolled stablewards before breakfast, as was my wont on most mornings at this time, for two new purchases had recently been made, and some of the old horses had just been taken up and were being put into work. Of the two come in, the led one was handed over to a strapper with the curt command, issued like a sergeant-instructor's order, by Batters, head stableman, "Pit this yin inna the lowse box," while he himself tied the other one up to a ring in a bare stall. I watched him run the stirrup irons up to the top of the leathers, loosen the girths to the first hole, raise the saddle up several times before settling it on the mare's back, take off his coat, and start to scrape her and wipe her over with a wisp of rough straw.

"Good morning, Batters," said I; "what do you think of her?"

Batters bit the straw in his mouth short before replying.

"Gude mornin', sir. A think she micht grow intil a beast some day; ony wey, A think A could mak' a beast o' her throu' time," which, being interpreted, meant, "In my opinion she'll do."

With this I was fain to be satisfied, and felt relieved, for I had bought the mare, an Irish five-year-old, without his opinion and advice, and dreaded the consequences of his disapproval.

After a pause, Batters added, "There's a telegraph on the road up for ye, sir," by which I understood that a telegraph message was in process of conveyance by the usual medium, the village postmistress, a lady of over thirty seasons' running, and broken to ride her bicycle barely twelve months ago.

"Did you not take the message from her?"

"A did note, becuz the mere was a wee feered

for the machine, an' A couldna ha'e taen't binna oo had baith gotten doon, an' the twa whulps hed follit mi i' the cuipples an' they micht ha'e rin amang her legs, an' mair as that, the wumman said there wuz a answer wantit till the telegraph."

Whereupon I returned to the house in search of the wumman and the "telegraph," whom I presently found. From a sort of reverie I was roused by the voice of Joanna saying, "The tele-girl is waiting to take the reply, and the puppies have already eaten the envelope and are attacking her bicycle. Is there any reply?"

Joanna knew there was, for, as she afterwards explained, she saw me extract the prepaid form from its cover, and she wondered what caused the wide grin to spread over my countenance; but she wished to be enlightened and consulted in the matter.

"Yes, there is a reply—an answer obvious—a question, in fact, as follows: 'Would I if offered accept a first-class ticket to Elysium?'"

We watched the so-called tele-girl wending her way down the drive on her solid-tyred bike, crawling across the bridge as if on a tortoise race, and disappearing round the bend of the road; and we wondered if the message, carefully read out and spelled over to her, had created any emotion other than that of pity in her stolid breast.

Then Joanna said, "Well?"

I spread the crumpled pink paper out on my knee. "No, 'Playmate,' down, 'Pastime,' you don't get this document to eat." It read: "Would you if offered take on the Forest fox-hounds as huntsman and master. Reply," and this over the name Gideon Dodd, one of the grandest old sportsmen in the whole Borderland. Again and again did I gaze at the electrifying message, and each time it brought up new sensations of delight in the attempt to realise what it meant. Fox-hounds, Huntsman, Master, Forest; each word costing one halfpenny to transmit, yet worth untold gold to me. I set out for a long stroll on the hillside to try and picture something of what it conveyed. It meant the acquiring one of the most sporting and useful little packs of fox-hounds in Britain: sporting, because it was hunted entirely without professional assistance, the Master carrying the horn and being assisted by two non-professional whips; and useful, because although only established some six years previously, it was already doing good work and killing foxes, and improving the sport obtained by neighbouring packs. It meant the serious business of providing and showing sport in a thoroughly sporting district; living in a community of sports men and women who had all the fire and energy of the old moss-troopers, and who, from childhood, were at home in the saddle; fond of a good horse and a good hound, and eager to enjoy to the full the pleasure of a good chase. It meant the interesting effort of breeding hounds, and the engrossing anxiety of bringing them forward; the delight of taking hounds of one's own breeding into the field; the satisfaction of seeing them take to hunting naturally as to the manner born; and the fascinating occupation of hunting hounds and studying hound-work.

It entailed a heap of time, labour, forethought, and craft, and the assuming all the heavy responsibility and the multifarious duties connected with the office of Mastership. Well might a more qualified person pause and hesitate; but in one thing I was not deficient, and that was keenness; and I knew I should get every support from a ready and willing staff, and from an enthusiastic field of followers. In old Batters—not that he was old in years, but in wisdom and experience—I had a tower of strength. A better stableman never existed. Punctual as the sun, and as early a riser, his knowledge of the constitution and temperament of his horses was very complete. For years he had turned out a small stud to do, and do well, the work of twice its number. Plenty of exercise, good strapping and dressing, very regular and frequent feeding and not too much corn at a time, was his practice. He hated "Vets," and except for surgical operations resented their being called in as a reflection on his own knowledge; and when this was proposed he used to mutter: "If oo sterve the horse an' pit a clean divot in his manger for him ti worry at, he'll turn better far quicker wantin' the Veet." A tyrant, but a just one, over the many stable lads that had passed through his hands, he had turned out some first-rate men whose recommendation was, they had been "an 'ear wi' auld Batters." He never quite forgave his master for inadvertently entering him in some official return as "Coachman." "A micht hae been putten doon what A am shairly—Stud-gruim." This description he would fairly earn now, for he was not slow in acquainting me with the stipulation that "there wad need ti be nae drievin' on huntin' days, an' that Johnny, his son, wad need ti be putten inta leevery, for he was lairnin' him ti drieve." The fact that a move would be made back into his native district, where he was a recognised authority and indeed looked on as a sort of oracle, would, I knew, reconcile him to any extra work and irregular hours which his new duties might bring.

With the hounds went a Volunteer First Whip, Tom Telfer; and no hunt possessed a more active or harder working one, a quicker man in the field, or more determined across a rough difficult country. His incursions to the larger neighbouring hunts were frequent and always brought fun of some kind, for he had a posse of followers who frequently got into difficulties in their attempts to follow him.

For the position of Second Whip I knew there would be some competition. In fact, there was some danger of the supply exceeding the demand. The anxiety of the field to assist during the progress of a fox chase was always superabundant, and on one occasion so great had been this eagerness that my predecessor is said to have declared that having run a dead-beat fox into a small plantation clear of rabbit-holes and all other refuges, he was the only man who was not hunting the hounds. So it was fixed that Jack Purdie, the head stable lad under Batters, should be appointed Second Whip and Second Horseman combined.

Over and over again that day did I enact in anticipation the joy of waving hounds into cover, and after a long chase, of course at a terrific pace over a big country, I pictured myself standing in the middle of the baying pack and throwing the dead body of a stiff fox to hounds. Coming in an hour later for lunch, I was asked by the lady who presides

HOW THE NEWS CAME

at the end of my table what I had been doing, and I replied, "Why, huntin' hounds, of course." To which she retorted, "If you are going to drop your 'g's' about like that I shan't play."

Later on in the day, Billy Kerr, a young relative, arrived breathless with excitement, and gasped out: "Is it true? For if it is, by the powers, I'll whip to you if you have only a three-legged horse to give me."

"Come away down to the stables, and I'll show you a four-legged one."

When the linen sheet was stripped from the Irish mare in obedience to Batters' command, "Peel that mere," and after her legs had been felt, and her hocks examined, the Oracle remarked, "She wadna mak' a bad wheep's horse, Maister Willyum."

As there had been no opportunity for an interchange of news between the two, it left it to be surmised that the tele-girl had revealed to Batters the momentous message of the morning.

"Let's have a look through what you've got here before I go," said Billy.

So the horses were inspected in turn with a new interest and a new importance, and much discussion took place as to whether this one or that one was suitable—fast enough, stout enough, and clever enough for a huntsman's horse.

"What have you just now?" asked Billy.

"At the moment there are five here and two at grass, seven hunters all told; all good of their kind, and all to be depended upon; but two of them are shared with the family."

"Which are these?"

"Well, there's 'Pepperbox,' whom you know—the 'Powney,' as Batters calls her, though she is 15.1½."

"Fifteen wan on her bare feet an' stannin' streetched," corrected that worthy.

"She's fresh as ever, and will come up from the grass firm and fat, and frisking like a filly."

"Yes," replied Bill, "she gives a very good imitation of Australian buck-jumping when the saddle is first laid on her, and a lot of fun to the man who crosses it. I remember our friend here had a convenient turn of lumbago last year, and gave me the privilege of 'first ride,'" he went on, seeing Batters leave the stable for a moment; "but I did not see much stiffness about him as he ran to catch her after she had disposed of me."

"The other is this one, one of that rare sort, anybody's horse, a very pleasant ride, an absolutely safe conveyance, a perfect fencer, and never sick or sorry; but, as Batters says, 'sair afflickit wi' want o' speed.'"

"This old arm-chair rather spoils the look of these three blood-like chasers," said Billy to Batters, who had come back.

"Mebbe she diz that, Captain Willyum, but she's yin o' the kind ye whiles read aboot but dinna aften see, an' she can mak' fules o' some o' the faster kind; an' what's mair," with a very steady and direct glance at his master, "she's a yuisfu' kind for a snawy day."

Thereupon I made a mental note that whether I wished it or not, "Old Safety" would have to remain in the Hunt stable.

"Ye'll never think o' pairtin' wi' the auld horse, sir,"

"Let's have one more look at the Irish mare."

continued Batters, after Bill had run his hand over old "Royal's" tendons and pinched his suspensory ligament, and had observed, "He stands over a bit more than I thought, and that flat foot doesn't improve, and he is a bit impetuous in a cramped country, is he not?"

"Put him away! Rather not, Bill. There's some three or four years' genuine work in him yet, and he and I will never part."

"The 'Pearl' here is another of the same, but faster, and has the advantage of youth, though she's not so careful where she puts her feet as I should like."

"What's this, Master?" as we came to a little thick dark-brown mare, with well-turned quarters, muscular thighs, and good straight hocks.

"That's the 'Omega' mare, Bill, only rising five years old, active and clever as a kitten, but has a little to learn yet, and has rather too much action for a hunter."

"Shae'll never dae ti keep," muttered Batters, as he unbuckled the roller; "she can lift her legs high eneuch, but she sets them doon in the verra same bit again."

Billy could find no fault with the mare's shapes when she was stripped; but the evident anxiety of Batters to cover her up again left little time for a thorough examination, and when the rug and roller were being adjusted I whispered to my companion the explanation that the Oracle could not ride her, and that she was not a favourite with him.

"Let's have one more look at the Irish mare," said Billy. So we had her run out, and picked her to pieces.

"How's she bred? I suppose you got a pedigree with her?"

"Yes, a real Irish pedigree; by 'Royal Meath' from 'Alanna,' and going back as long as your arm, and a reputation even longer."

"Yes; what was it the dealer said about her?"

"Well, after I had bought the mare, and he had pocketed his cheque, I said, 'Now, Maloney, the mare is mine and not returnable; is there anything about her that I should know? Has she any trick in or out of the stable?' 'Thrick is it?' he replied, gulping down a glass of brown sherry which he had selected to wet the bargain. 'In the sthable she has a thrick av licking out her manger clane, an' out av the sthable she has a thrick av takin' ye to the front an' keepin' ye there.' Then warming up, he went on, 'Whei, the lasht toime I rode her misilf wid the fox-hounds, we had a twilve-moile point, an' she finished wan iv twilve others in a field av siventy. On our way home we met the sthag-hounds jist startin', so as she was quite fresh, I tuk her on. We ran a twinty moile point this toime—only foive of us finished out av a field av a hundred,' and, raising his voice to a high scream, 'an' wan av thim foive was your mare.'"

When Bill had done laughing, he said, "Well, I must mount my hireling and tak' the road."

"I suppose Brockie, of Kelso, has some useful hack-hunters, eh, Batters?"

"Him," said Batters, in a tone of inexpressible contempt, "him: no, he hez nae horse."

"But I saw at least a dozen standing there to-day."

"Weel, he hez twae'r three auld rungs aboot the place that he thinks is horses; but he hez nae horse."

"But this one I'm riding to-day is not a bad old screw."

"Weel," persisted Batters, "there's a broon mare he bocht at Bosills Fair. Ye micht get a canny half-day's work oot o' her if ye didna pussh her ower sair, and him, ye micht ca' him a beast; but forbye them twae, the feck o' them's auld rungs."

CHAPTER II

TAKING THEM OVER

" To rear, feed, hunt, and discipline the pack."
—SOMERVILE.

FOLLOWING close upon this memorable morning, preliminaries were quickly arranged, and it was agreed to take over the hounds at once, and bring them to temporary summer quarters at a hill farm, while the permanent premises were being put ready for them.

After spending several days with the retiring huntsman, drinking in the flow of his advice, hanging upon his every utterance, and fearful of forgetting the slightest tip imparted in the boiling-shed or sleeping-house, where nearly every minute of the time was passed, the move was made.

Tom the feeder in front, a new and proud huntsman next, Jack the second whip and Billy flanking, and Jock the kennel terrier strutting at the head of the pack, formed the light-hearted cavalcade as we left at 6 A.M. one fine cool morning. The roads were nicely damped for hounds' feet, a condition which Tom took credit for obtaining by special stipulation with the weather regulator. Tom had no world outside and beyond the confines of his kennel, and seemed to think that all things existed for or against the well-being of his beloved hounds.

An hour's jog brought us to a river, the boundary of the Forest country proper, which we crossed at a shallow ford, five or six miles below a manufacturing town. Horses would not drink the coloured water; but most of the hounds drank freely, and some were sick immediately afterwards. Tom's remark upon the occasion was characteristic of the man: "Stinkin' fellahs them malefacterers puttin' all that dye-stuff into the water—might ha' known it would sicken hounds."

Three hours later, of which half the time led over a moorland track, we sighted a snug farmhouse in the heart of the hills, and took possession of the extemporised kennels. An old smearing-shed had been converted into two sleeping-houses, with a boiling-house and a small feeding-yard behind, and a large grass yard with a stream of water running through it in front. We put hounds on to their benches, and gazed at them for some time; and one satisfied soul felt that a new era had commenced.

What an interest life had during the next few weeks, and how full the days were. Bustle and activity reigned, and few idle moments were passed; and what enjoyment the novelty and excitement brought. The early rising, the canter across the moor in the crisp air to the kennels, the long trails among the glorious hills to condition horse and hound, the feeding of the hounds and calling them over, and all the kennel work, the doctoring feet and ears, the loafing on the green in the afternoons, getting acquainted with the character and disposition of individual hounds, the playing with the puppies, all made the days pass like a midsummer dream.

The puppies were soon made handy in the couples, and shortly after this their ears were rounded. This operation was performed by the huntsman of a neighbouring pack, who, by special favour, rode over to do it, and brought two couple of draft hounds with him as an offering of goodwill, and to strengthen our pack.

It was a noteworthy day, and every effort had been made in the kennels to have things in apple-pie order; and the great man was pleased to express his approval, and to say, "We looked a very useful lot." His remark as to the new huntsman, afterwards passed on to me, was: "I daresay he'll hunt the hounds well enough, quite as well as any amature." He gave many valuable hints, one of the chief being: "The first day you hunt be sure to choose a place where you are certain of finding cubs, and where there is no riot. Blood your young hounds if possible; but above all get them to smell him and chase him. To run a hot *blowing* fox before they kill him is more important for young hounds than the actual killing; the worry often frightens them till they know what it is."

Episode the first was the eating of Peter Amos, the shepherd's, favourite cat. Hounds would not look at the cats about the farm steading, and indeed two or three lived in the kennels and used to steal meat out of the feeding troughs. But this one invited its fate, for one early morning it pounced on a young rabbit and carried it off, trotting along the road in front of us for two or three hundred yards, as we returned from exercise. Old Peter guessed what had happened, for his favourite was missed from its daily custom of bringing in rabbits, leverets, and young game birds to its "kittlins," so to clear the atmosphere we introduced the subject on the first opportunity.

"Peter, there's rather too many cats about the place just now."

No reply.

"It's all very well to have a few to keep down the vermin, but when they get beyond a few, they are apt to get into trouble."

Still no reply.

"In fact, any cat seen a mile away from home will have to be destroyed."

Then Peter, with a stern face and a hard voice: "For ma pairt A wud raither keep cāāts az rāāts," and wheeled and strode away.

One of the old draft hounds was the principal offender in this instance, and as he distinguished himself soon after in a way calculated to bring discredit on the pack, his death warrant was signed. We had ridden over (with hounds) to a farm which seemed a likely walk for a puppy. We had shut hounds up in the straw-barn, and were interviewing old Mr. Brydon in his parlour. He had just said: "I didna ken hoonds were sic bonny massy beasts, and I wud like fine ti rear a whulp; but the mistress——"

Billy was eloquently urging that Mrs. B. need know no fear, two whelps were no trouble, that one kept the other out of mischief, and so on; when we both saw passing the window that gluttonous fiend "Forager" with the carcase of a hen hanging from his jaws, and pursued by another couple who were grabbing at the dainty morsel, and strewing feathers all over the lawn. Billy ran out, and I did my best to hold the worthy couple in conversation, and had to assent to a second glass of very fiery whisky to accomplish this, touching on every topic from the price and condition of ewes to the prospects of harvest, and keeping one eye on the window and the other on Mr. B.'s glass the while. Shortly afterwards I made an escape, leaving the crime unconfessed, and, as we believed, undetected. Mr. Brydon's last words were: "I'll think aboot the maitter o' the whulp."

Billy's account was that when he got to the straw-barn he found the two lads throwing half-mangled corpses of fowls down the pit of the mill-wheel, and smothering clouds of feathers in the straw. Some luckless hens had been roosting on the rafters; and when the door was closed on the pack, they had flown down in the darkness, and courted certain death.

No puppies were taken to walk by Mr. and Mrs. Brydon that year.

About this time Billy went off rather suddenly and with much mystery, as he only revealed "he was going south." Two days later we received two incomprehensible wires from him, the first reading, "*Have bought her;*" the second, though handed in an hour before the first, received an hour later, and reading, "*Have seen A Clinker. Carrie is a lady.*" Of course, Joanna instantly composed several replies to the effect that we were interested to have his

"Forager" with the carcase of a hen hanging from his jaws.

opinion as to the gentle birth of Carrie, and pleased that he had seen Mr. Clinker, and that if he contemplated bringing one or both back with him she had only one spare room at present; but dreading the complications that mutilation of the message might produce, and grudging the 4s. 6d. involved in sending, none of them were sent. In the end of the week Billy returned with the Clinker, a grey thoroughbred, five-year-old mare; but without the suggested lady, at whose non-appearance, after having had her explained away to our dull minds, Joanna professed profound disappointment.

A DAY IN THE KENNELS

When Billy asked blandly, "May I bring John Elliot to see hounds fed to-morrow, and his sister with him?" I already knew from my usual source of information that he had written asking the lady to come with her brother to lunch, and to see hounds fed, and had received a reply that she would be charmed. So as we strolled along the footpath leading to the kennels next afternoon, I contrived to appropriate the young lady in spite of Billy's manœuvres, and found her delightfully naïve and refreshing. Before reaching the kennels, Miss Florence having heard that we had some cubs in captivity, asked to see them. They were in a newly built pig-house that had never been occupied, and the surroundings were quite sanitary and wholesome. There was a small quantity of hay in a corner of the inside house, and the yard was covered over with wire netting. Tom the feeder used to look after them, but beyond throwing in a rabbit or a crow occasionally, he did not keep them as he kept his hounds' quarters. Miss Florence was a very dainty young lady, and as she tip-toed up wind to the courtyard she suddenly came to a dead stop, holding her nose.

"Shall I go in and stir them up?" said Billy.

"Oh no, please don't; I don't think I'd care to see them."

As we walked away she said, "Mr. Master, I used to think it so clever of fox-hounds to smell a fox and so far off, and wondered how they did it. I don't wonder at all now."

Clad in linen coats, and taking an ash plant in our hands, we entered the boiling-house, and at a crucial moment. Tom was standing on a wooden stool over a thirty-gallon boiler filled with hot bubbling porridge, and stirring with a wooden weapon like a canoe paddle, as if his life depended on his labour, and he barely noticed us. He then jumped down and raked out the glowing coals from the fire-box of the furnace, and was joined by Jack, who had been mincing up junks of boiled horse-flesh with a chopper.

"Keep the puddin' movin' for a bit yet, Jack. The copper is nearly red hot."

Florence looked on with great interest, and had many questions to ask.

"Do they eat all that to-day? Do you give it them hot like that? Does that last them for a week?"

She was instructed that this was the feed for to-morrow and next day, and we watched the men ladle it out with big scoops into wooden coolers, from which the boiling of two days previous had been

TAKING THEM OVER

cut out with a spade in solid cubes, which looked most appetising in the troughs in the feeding-house next door.

"Let's take hounds out on the green while the pudding is being prepared," suggested Bill.

As hounds climbed round one, and scrambled and raced for a little bit of broken biscuit thrown to them, my volunteer whip got the ear of the young lady for a time, and had evidently been impressing her with his knowledge of hounds' names, for she said to me, " Do you know that Mr. Kerr knows all the hounds' names," and added shyly, " Do you ? "

I was obliged to confess I did, and disclaiming any supernatural talent for the accomplishment, continued, " There is a shepherd here who knows at a glance every one of the 640 sheep he has to look after." But this did not seem to impress Miss Florence as much as might have been expected.

"Feeding-time, Tom ? " as that individual appeared at the kennel door. "Very well, now let's see you separate the puppies first."

"Right, sir. Stand back, hounds: steady there now: then, puppies, little puppies, puppies *only;* here, little boys; here, little dearies:" and in no time he had six couple of young hounds forward wriggling with delight; and while the old hounds all remained standing dejected in the background, they were allowed to pick out the tit-bits. Then a little more flesh and biscuits was added, and the old hounds called over singly, the shy feeders first—Dainty, Lavender, Beeswing, Rosalind, Pilgrim, Woodman, Ringwood, Gossamer, Gambol, Dexter, Sportsman, Ranter, Dalesman, Driver, Newsman.

Then, after a pause, as fast as they could be named—Warrior, Trywell, Trojan, Templar, Truthful, Dewdrop, Ringlet, Ruffian, Regent, Proctor, Rallywood, Royal, Talisman, Rustic, Challenger, Marmion, Pirate, Lapwing, Tyrant.

In a very short time the troughs were cleared out and polished clean, and hounds started to lick each other all over.

"What are these poor things, Tom?" inquired Miss Florence, as three hounds—Forager, Chorister, Wisdom—were let out of a small shed to join the others.

"Them three, Missus, is to have ile to-night" ("Because they've been naughty," ejaculated Billy, bursting with laughter), "and I'm preparing them for it. Besides, old Forager will lick about a full feed off the muzzles and backs to the others."

As we were leaving, some little kittens appeared from below the meal-chest on the concrete floor.

"They were kittened underneath there," explained Tom.

"You'd better put an old sack or something for them to lie on."

"Oh, sir, when they feel cold they lie on the porridge," retorted Tom; and sure enough I frequently saw them after this extended flat on their little stomachs, their hind feet pushed out behind them, evidently enjoying the comfort of the heat-retaining pudding.

Old Batters was a man of moods. He was either tiresomely taciturn or abundantly voluble; and we could never decide in which he showed to the greater advantage. He had often to be consulted on matters outside and not pertaining to the stables, and indeed was never slow to give his opinion or present a theory when asked. He was in his loquacious mood as he drove me back from the last train one evening about this time, and introduced the subject of a projected servants' dance.

"Na, na," he emphatically declared, "A wadna hev nae drink—drink disna dae whan there's females aboot."

He was equally firm as to the undesirability of including a certain youth in the list of invited guests. This individual was a musician and a step-dancer, and had been in great request till his habits drove people to be rather shy of him.

"It wad never dae to hev Yeddy Da'gleish," said the Oracle. "Ye see the warst o' him is whan he gets on, he strikes; no like Donal' Purdie, for he juist roars when he gets drink, and Sandy Blyth he juist glowers an' grumphs. Yedd got on at Talla sports a week past on Setterday an' strak. Oo was kinda coaxin' him awa', an' oo had gotten 'im as fer as the brig, when he brak awa' frae us an' made straicht for the tent and strak. The sairgent tell't mi the poliss wasna for lifting onybody frae the sports; but Yedd he strak that sair an' that wicked they couldna evite it, so they juist liftit um."

After a very brief silence, which he broke only by an abortive hiccup, Batters went off at a tangent.

"Hev they gotten thae Boors oot o' the camp on yon river yet? Hes Sir Buller won ower yet, sir?"

"No, not yet; but Sir Redvers is getting up his guns to shell them out."

"Weel, I'll tell ye what should be dune—what A

wad dae if they askit me—what A think they shood dae: they shood juist keep blatterin' on at them nicht an' day."

After several more oracular utterances, and before the house-lights appeared, I began to think I preferred Batters' taciturn mood.

When he had received the instructions for next day, and before driving off to the stables, he whispered mysteriously that he had seen "the best shapit horse" in the countryside that evening at Brockie's livery stables while waiting for the train.

"He's a graund tappit yin, an' a graund middle't yin, an' the finest leggit yin, wi' the best per o' fower legs—the best set o' fower legs—A ever clappit een on. Short cannon banes, an' hocks ner the grund, nerrer as ony A ever saw; in fack his hocks is *on the grund*." He then blew into my ear: "He micht be bocht for a hunder." Almost in the same breath he groaned: "Dinna buy that mere o' Maister Willyum's."

Expressing a desire to have an opportunity of inspecting the phenomenal horse, and disclaiming all desire to possess the grey mare, I for the third and last time wished him good-night.

CHAPTER III

A MORNING'S EXERCISE

"*Then on the sunny bank they roll and stretch
  Their dripping limbs, or else in wanton rings
  Coursing around, pursuers and pursued;
  The merry multitudes disporting play.*"
—SOMERVILE.

THE grey mare was turning out fairly well, but she had much to learn. She was being schooled to stand the whip, and was also being regularly ridden on the moor to train her to avoid putting her feet in sheep drains, of which she knew nothing when she first came. She had one very bad fault, which was to run back directly she felt the toe in the stirrup. Billy was very patient with her, and gentled her up to a certain point, and if this failed he adopted a stronger method. His endearing epithets were numerous. He would begin by "Gently then, my little lady;" "Gently now, my bonnie sweetheart;" "Woe ho, my pet beauty, woe ho." Then, as the mare moved backwards, he would tap her behind the fore-legs and say, "Stand still, will you;" "Stand still, you wild wench;" "Stand still, you lanky jade;" "Stand still, you long-legged besom." Being a man of resource, he tied up a fore-foot, and used to spend hours swinging his own long leg up and down, and practising mounting from the off side, at which he soon became an adept. Lastly, he formed a sort of crush—a narrow pen of two palings ended by a stiff prickly holly bush—inside of which enclosure he pushed her, and swung confidently into the saddle. This first experiment was more than successful, for the mare backed against the bush and then shot forward so suddenly and with such force, that she jerked her rider behind the saddle, and then getting a slight chuck in the mouth she got up on end and slid the astonished horseman not ungracefully over her tail, to the unconcealed delight of the few privileged onlookers. The "jade" got clear, and after cutting up the tennis lawn, was only captured at the stable door. The gentling method was taken up again, and proved successful, for she was soon pronounced "whip quiet," and "steady to mount."

It was about this time that Billy made a half-hearted approach to pass on the "Clinker" to the Hunt stable, at a profit of course.

"Are you sure you have plenty horses to start with, old man?" he began. "These hill fellows are terrible keen, and even two days a week, with an occasional five days a fortnight, will take some doin' in that country. I hear they are accustomed to hounds drawing on till dark, whatever they may have done in the mornin'. 'Twould never do to start with too few."

I explained that I was in the enviable position of only being required to horse myself, that my first whip found his own horses, and that the second whip really did second horseman's work only, as there was never any trouble with hounds not coming on or being left out; that five horses

She slid the astonished horseman not ungracefully over her tail.

keeping sound would easily do the work, and reminded him that I had five, not counting the little mare that old Batters called the "Powney," and which had never been known to tire or fall. Then came a feeler.

"My mare is going awfully nicely with Jack (second horseman) just now; she'll make a clinking hunter."

"I thought she was that already," said I.

Then after a pause, as if speaking to himself: "I've a mind to do a swop with Jack Elliot; he's half a stone lighter than I am, and his mare, though not so fast as mine, is up to a stone more weight;" and continued, "I think you'd like her if you once rode her, and I'm only asking a tenner more than I paid for her."

To which I answered, "No, no, Bill, I don't buy unmade ones, and never one made or unmade from a pal. Swop with Jack Elliot if you like, but don't try to shunt her on to me."

Next morning he said, after our return from exercise, "I say, old man, I'm awfully glad you didn't buy my mare off me last night," than which nothing had been more remote from my intention.

This abortive deal partly but not wholly prepared me for Jack Elliot's question a few days later.

"Are you really trying to buy Bill Kerr's mare?" I looked encouragingly at him, and he went on. "For if you are, I'll stand out till the deal is done or off. He says you are awfully sweet on her."

I was petrified to hear this, though I managed to conceal my amazement, and more than amused when it came round to me later that the young ruffian had added, "She takes a little bit of riding, and between ourselves, I don't think that she is exactly his mare."

That morning's exercise had been productive of several small incidents. Billy had returned to the slumbering house, under the pretext of getting his pipe, after we started, and had taken off his hat to a lightly draped figure at an upper window, which he did with so much action as to make the mare shy off, and he dropped his pipe on the gravel. He got down to pick it up, and found that the lesson of the holly bush had been, temporarily at least, forgotten, for directly he put his foot into the stirrup, and before he could swing up, the "Clinker" began her old trick of running backwards and spinning round. No man looks his best in the difficult and humiliating position of hopping on a straightened leg after a gyrating horse, the other foot being wedged firmly home in the stirrup three feet or more from the ground. Bill was aware of this, but kept his head admirably, though a chuckle of laughter came from behind the curtain of the open window. He was mindful of his experience of the slide over the tail, and let the reins lie perfectly loose, and waiting his chance till the moment of a slight lull in the top-like movement, he took a big handful of mane and swung into the saddle. The mare darted off like a released bird, and before he caught his stirrup she had done a good half-mile at racing speed.

Not long after leaving kennels we came across the stale drag of a night-wandering fox, for some of the old hounds, after feeling about with noses on the ground, darted out, and stooping to it, would soon have carried it on. But the vigilant Jack was round

A MORNING'S EXERCISE 27

them in an instant, and swinging his whip with "Warrior, leave it there; get over and leave it, Pilgrim," while Billy chimed in, the two soon had the pack clustering round the old mare's heels. So on we went for a couple of hours, now walking, now jogging, till we came to a knoll covered with short heather. There we got down and spent half-an-hour letting hounds roll and push and draw themselves along on their backs and sides to their full content, and tossing bits of biscuit to the puppies.

"Let's have a practice at the horn, Master," said Billy. Whereupon he blew a blast with more vehemence than harmony. Old "Safety" ran backward with fright, the Irish mare wheeled round with the whip, the old hounds raised their ears and looked puzzled, and the young hounds dropped their sterns and prepared for flight; in fact, Playmate made off, dragging old Marmion, to whom he was coupled, for some distance before he stopped. The sheep on the opposite hillside drew together in alarm, and I now knew what old Peter the shepherd meant this morning. He had told me: "A couldna' jaloose what had gliffed the sheep off the hicht yestreen. A faund the hill-end cut a' hotted thigether in a batt when A cam' roun' the hill." My volunteer whip had stolen out to the hilltop to have a "practice on the horn."

And some of the morning's incidents were of an amusing nature. A little way beyond our halting place we suddenly came upon a most patriarchal-looking billy-goat tethered by a long rope to a stout stake. Some of the young hounds were scared, and seemed inclined to bolt, but most of them appeared to wish a closer inspection. Two or three had fallen behind. Jack went back to put them on, cracking his whip as I called encouragingly to them. This had the effect of starting the goat off at a fast canter, which he kept up round and round in ever-lessening circles till he had wound himself up close to his post, where, stamping and butting, he looked most formidable, with Ruffian, Pilgrim, and Pirate baying at him. It took several smart cuts with the whip to drive them off, and my laughter did not diminish when Billy said, "By Jove, I do believe they would not have been long in breaking up old Nebuchadnezzar. Tell ye what, if we don't find a fox first day out we might enlarge the patriarch on the top of Blue Cairn; believe they'd run the high old boy with half a day's start."

These exercising "trails," as Batters called them, were a great delight at the time, and a most pleasant recollection to recall—the whole surroundings were so attractive and picturesque, and it was all so satisfying. At the same time we looked forward with an eagerness that almost amounted to impatience to the rapidly approaching time when we should start work.

"When do you intend to begin business, Master?" was the question frequently put by my supernumerary whip, and repeated this morning as we turned our horses' heads homewards. It was explained to him that the hill country would only stand three or four days' hunting at most, that though cubs had been seen we could not be sure they had not moved on, and that in our own country proper, where we proposed to move shortly, corn would not be cut for two or three weeks yet.

A MORNING'S EXERCISE

On one of the first days of September the usual question was put, supplemented by the observation, "Look at the muscles on hounds' backs and thighs, and see how fit horses are."

"Yes; but we must have a few more days on the roads to harden hounds' feet, and one or two more of these long trails on the hill tracks will be of great benefit to horses' legs."

"Horses' legs are hard and clean, and old 'Safety' is getting quite conceited" (referring to an unexpected wallop the old mare had given some mornings ago, and which had put me on to her neck).

I took no notice of Bill's last remark, and replied, "Yes, legs are good; that's the cool wet grass knee-high acting as a cold-water bandage, and the absence of concussion in these soft hill tracks. They must have some more of it, and get on to faster work and have a pipe opener or two before they are fit to begin business, as you put it; but perhaps the week after next, if it comes rain."

I saw Billy's suction get a little stronger, and great volumes of smoke came from his half-extinguished pipe, and he vented his feelings by putting his heels into his mare's sides, which caused her to jump forward almost on the top of some coupled hounds.

At late breakfast he said, through a mouthful of cold grouse pie, "I don't know which part of it I like best, it's all so splendid and wholesome."

Joanna and I exchanged glances, for this was the exact description given of Billy himself lately, and it fitted him precisely.

"I think I know," said the lady, as she drew the oatcakes and honey from his reach; "but really, you must put on the muzzle if you wish to get anywhere near the hounds when they run by-and-by."

"A man can't work for nothing; you surely don't grudge me two light meals a day, with a snack between times?"

"It's the snacks I do grudge," replied the housekeeper, wistfully eyeing about half a pound of honeycomb being transferred to his plate.

As I was looking through my letters, Billy, who had been down to the stables to see how much of her oats the grey mare had left, for amongst other faults she was a shy feeder, reported, "There's a character in the saddle-room; you'd better go down and see him."

"Who is he, Bill?"

"Oh, go and see for yourself; I think he'll amuse you."

After finishing my correspondence, I went down, and was surprised to see a figure which I took to be Batters, in an unimpeachable Sunday suit of clothes, sitting on a stool silently smoking. He never moved, and scarcely appeared to breathe, so somewhat mystified, I said in a half whisper, "Batters."

"Coming, sir," said that worthy from the adjoining stable, and when he appeared the resemblance to the motionless figure was still more apparent. "A was stertin' to rasp that grey mare's teeth; that's ma faither, sir."

Batters looked any age between thirty and sixty, but was much nearer the latter age, and the figure on the stool looked considerably younger as it sat; but on being spoken to it solemnly dropped from the stool on to the shortest and bandiest pair of legs that ever curled round a saddle flap, removed the pipe from its mouth, and sticking it behind its ear, stood at attention.

"He's just ridden a colt over from Sir William Miller's to see the Irish mare," went on Batters, junior, "and he'll be starting back directly."

"You've had a long ride," I said.

"Parteeklar, sir," was the reply.

"How do you like the mare?"

"Parteeklar, parteeklar, sir."

"Come up to the house before you go."

"Parteeklar, parteeklar, parteeklar, sir."

The old fellow soon after appeared, part and parcel of his horse, at the door. Billy had offered him cherry brandy, saying to me, "Perhaps it may make him diversify his dialogue," and the old chap with a brightening eye assented, believing he was being offered brandy. He eyed the ruby liquid very suspiciously, and would have smelled it had he been unobserved. Then taking a very small sip, he said, "Parteeklar;" another sip—"No bad;" sip—"Gey guid;" sip—"Dode, that's better nor whusky;" a large sip— "A body wad never sta' onna that;" a final gulp— "Yin could juist drink that till yin fell aneth the table."

"True," laughed Billy, "that will set you up for the ride home. How far is it."

"Parteeklar, sir, thirty mile," the old boy responded, as he started at a hound's jog pace down the avenue.

"Well, that beats anything I ever heard in the Forest country last week," roared Bill; and after dinner that night he related some of his experiences on that occasion. He had repaired thither with his mare, partly on his own business, and partly on that of the Hunt. I had deputed him to see how the work at the new kennels was progressing, to call on prospective puppy walkers, to see some of the farmers and learn when harvest was likely to be over, and to carry out many such, to him, congenial errands. His projected two nights away had been extended to a week. He had had two days' grouse-shooting, two days' trout-fishing, one lazy day (Sunday of course), and two days at business, staying most of the time with the Elliots, and he came home wearing one of Jack Elliot's shirts and carrying one of Miss Flo's pocket-handkerchiefs. He had deferred meeting some of the hunting men till his last day (market day), and had a heavy time, and on his return complained of headache.

"Look here, Master," he said, "if you want to drink even with some of those old Johnnies over in the Forest country, you'll have to begin to harden a bit. I was boxed up yesterday with three or four old topers; one a coursing man, one a famous curler, and one a gamekeeper, and all keen fox-hunters. The last was hale and hearty, and took his liquor straight, while the others were gulping and shirking and spilling it, while I was sitting tight scarcely daring to move. Old Cherry-trees asked M'Alister the keeper, seventy-five if a day, 'George, how have ye kept yer health so well? What kind of rule did ye make about drink?' 'Weel, Jims,' old M'Alister returned, 'I made this rule early in life, an' I follit it a' thro': I drank whusky and naething but whusky every day up ti' sunset; then' (sinking his voice to a whisper) 'efter sunset—brandy.'"

Old Dykes the coursing farmer told that so far as he knew only one of the young hounds at walk had come to grief, and that by being run over by a loaded cart, about which the guid-wife was heart-broken, and had that very day written me a letter imploring me to send her another whelp. Dykes also told, through many hiccups, how his own puppy, in fighting with a young greyhound bitch for the coveted honour of sleeping across the foot of his cook's bed, had bitten her ("the sapling, not the wummin," Dykes interjected) through the eye to the loss of its sight. When sympathised with, and asked by Billy if he would not like to send the puppy in, the old fellow replied, "Oh, never heed, I wadna like to want the whulp or lambing comes in, an' he'll mebbe no dae't again."

All these quaint characters he had met, and the evidences of the sportsmanlike tendencies of the people had made a great impression on Billy, who kept going over his experiences again and again, and deploring the fact that he had not made earlier acquaintance with them. He had seen Tom Telfer, our official first whip, itching for the appearance of the pack in the field, and had met for the first time Sandy Oliver, master of a south side of the Border Hunt, a man for whom cleuchs and sykes and bogs, and mosses, and well-eyes, and hidden sheep drains, and swollen burns, and treacherous fords had no terrors, and who was at home amongst the hills on the blackest night and in the wildest snow-drift.

He also came across a daft soul, Will Phaup o' the Wisp. In a rough prolonged hill chase this individual, a great breeder of rams and of a few horses as well, was undefeated. He had pulled out a well-shaped but rather backward three-year-old for inspection, and was told it looked short of condition.

"I never like them rolling fat to start the season," he stated.

"But you're never going to hunt that beast; I was going to ask if he was broken to lead," Billy had said.

"Broken to lead," shrieked Will Phaup; "man, I hunted him last season three days in the same week in the foremost flight."

"But, Will, that's no way to treat a young one."

"I ken, lad, but the auld mare was lame, and when the hoonds come whoopin' and hollerin' round yer verra door, what's a man to dae?"

We smoked and talked, and talked and smoked again till far past midnight, and Billy was knocking the ashes from his pipe preparatory to telling of Andrew Waugh, "the very finest old boy of the lot," when a summons from the bed-room overhead was rapped out through the ceiling with such precision and vigour as to leave no doubt of its meaning, and the sitting was adjourned.

When I retired, a voice from the pillows asked, "Have you fixed upon a name for the grey mare yet?"

"Well, no, we didn't touch on the subject at all. Why?"

"Because he's been at me to suggest a name for his mare, and I've given him some most suitable ones—'Quicksilver,' 'Grey Nun,' and others; and I'm determined not to propose the one he wants, and you must not do so either."

"What does he want, and how do you know?"

"Why, stupid, 'Lady Florence' of course."

CHAPTER IV

A MORNING'S CUBBING

" *With nostrils opening wide, o'er hill, o'er dale*
  The vig'rous hounds pursue, with ev'ry breath
Inhale the grateful steam, quick pleasures sting
  Their tingling nerves, while they their thanks repay,
And in triumphant melody confess
  The titillating joy."—SOMERVILE.

"COME on, Maister! this is no time of day to lie sweltering in bed," said Billy's cheery voice.

It was 4.10 A.M. on the morning of our first cubbing, and swelter could barely be called an accurate description of my condition. For when I woke up half-an-hour previously, in time to stop the alarum clock from going off, I had looked out and had seen in the grey light a distinct rime on the grass, and felt the atmosphere more than chilly. But passing over this, I replied, "Thanks for waking me, Bill; please don't disturb the house, but slip downstairs and light up the coffee, like a good chap, and I'll be with you in two twos." When, half-an-hour later, I joined him at the stable door, he was stamping his feet, thumping his hands, and sucking impatiently at a black briar pipe.

When the horses, old "Safe Conveyance" and the grey mare, were led out, their thin summer coats stood up, their tails were tucked tight in, and their ears laid back; and when we got up and moved away they put their backs up and were ready to wriggle out from below us on the smallest excuse. We were soon all aglow with the canter across the moor to the farm, which we accomplished without incident, except the dropping of Billy's pipe.

The sight of hounds rushing out of kennel further quickened the circulation, and though old "Safety" usually stood their onset very steadily, she wheeled with such amazing rapidity that we nearly parted company, and I saw an ill-suppressed smile on Tom the feeder's face. Then reinforced by the two lads, we moved away.

Full of eager expectation, we jogged along towards the hills, not holding hounds up too closely. We first tried an old plantation of about six acres, not thoroughly well fenced off and rather bare of under cover, and got indications of a cold line here and there. The old hounds had feathered and tried hard to own it from time to time, and were desperately keen; they had tried every yard of it and came out readily to the voice, a little bit inclined to flash, but we soon had them in hand and proceeded to our next draw.

Imagine a thirty-year-old plantation, about sixteen acres in extent, of spruce and Scotch fir, with some unhealthy larches and a few hardwoods, chiefly ash and mountain-ash, all lichen-covered and wind-waved, some lying over and some laid flat by gales, of quadrangular shape, with sharp-pointed corners and slightly incurved sides, surrounded by an old fail dyke two and a half feet high, riddled with rabbit holes on two

A MORNING'S CUBBING

sheltered sides, and surmounted by two bars of rotten paling. Through it were patches where the trees were thick and bushy but stunted, and here the heather grew close and high, overhanging and covering the open drains that had been made to dry the mossy soil, and providing dry snug lying in all weathers. From one corner stretched a thick bed of reeds and dwarf willows, running out into a small moss, where water stood several feet deep during most of the year. This was the starting-point, which we approached with feelings not easily described.

Billy and Tom slipped forward to watch their respective corners as arranged, with repeated orders to hold the fox or foxes up in cover as long as they could, on no account to holloa the first fox away, and not to cheer to an old fox on pain of a double thonging.

Assisted by Jack and two young farmers, on fat sweating horses, who had turned up, we followed on, keeping hounds together. When within two or three hundred yards of cover, hounds broke away on a drag, and opened before they got to the wood, into which they hurled themselves.

In less time than it took to get forward, and before the young hounds had squeezed through the fence, Billy was screaming on the other side as if to burst his lungs, and hounds were crushing through the undergrowth in full chorus and pouring out at the far side. Billy made a faint attempt to ride across them in response to my yells of " Stop them, for pity's sake, stop them!" Then catching hold of his bridle and kicking his long-legged grey mare in the ribs, he humped his shoulders and sent her pounding away in pursuit.

"Why did you holler them away? Why didn't you stop them?" I shouted, when I got within earshot; "it can't be a cub."

"Don't know," replied he, in the tone of don't-want-to-know; "only saw his back as he crept along the bottom of the sheep drain."

Here was an unexpected start, and an undesired one: a hill fox with his nose to the hills, and hounds screaming close behind him on a hot scent, having had no work to draw for him, and no trouble to find him themselves, and the young hounds hanging back wondering what it was all about.

But see the sheep drawing together only a quarter of a mile in front; and "Jupiter! there he goes crossing back over the white moss and coming in; perhaps it's a cub after all." By riding inside of hounds as they swung left-handed we got nearer them, and to our joy saw them turn sharp back towards the cover we had just left. But to our dismay we heard them run right through without dwelling, saw them carry the line out on the far side, and things began to look serious as they streamed away a second time, with an increased cry and no slackening of speed, most of the puppies joining in this time.

Divided between a desperate desire to get forward to see which hounds were running at head, and to hang back and curse Billy, I galloped along towards the hills, the chorus getting fainter as hounds tailed out and sunk the wind. At first I kept in touch by riding the ridges, where the going was sound, and by keeping to some bridle tracks which I knew,

A MORNING'S CUBBING

and saw hounds crossing to the right front towards Billy, who was riding cunning on the off-side, and who now seemed likely to cut in. On looking round again, I saw the grey mare loose, floundering in soft ground, with her rider on his hands and knees, with a crumpled hat. He got up and ran helplessly after her as she gained sounder ground, and made for a corner in a cross-wire fence. To my horror she rose deliberately at it, and though ringing the top wire hard all round, she got over it and cantered off in a direction opposite to that in which the pack were vanishing.

Luckily I hit upon a gate, and then having little else as a guide than the terriers showing now and again like white specks on the heather, and sheep occasionally bunched together on the hillsides, I held on my way. I was making for a deep glen or linn in the heart of the hills, which ran at right angles to the line of the chase, for, knowing it to have at least two strong breeding earths besides numerous kennels and lying places on the rocky ledges and loose stones on both sides of the stream, I fully expected to find hounds here. Half-an-hour of bad going, during which there was no indication of them except the overtaking of two very tired and blown puppies, whose delight to see me was touching, brought me within hail of a shepherd. He shouted back in a high-pitched key that he had "seen hoonds rinnin' like mad oot by ayont the bunemaist scaur in the fore day." In the next half-mile occurred not the least catastrophe of the day, for in scrambling over a gap in the stone wall "Old Safety" cut herself badly. After washing and binding it up, the wound continued to bleed considerably, so there was nothing for it but to go back home with her. Seven miles took an hour and a half to do, when at eleven o'clock I again set out on a fresh horse to look for the pack.

I found one hound near where I had turned back, evidently working homewards on the back trail, which confirmed the shepherd lad's information, and jogging along for another six miles towards a large woodland in enclosed country, a gamekeeper gave the news that a certain young farmer had got hold of the hounds, had taken them on to his farm and shut them up in his straw barn. There I found them a little footsore, and one couple only short, and heard Paton's story.

At about 10.30 A.M. he was riding in to the market town. While off his horse to open a gate on the edge of the moor, he saw a fox crossing a grass field. Not dreaming of hounds, and seeing the fox was very tired, he kept perfectly still and watched. The animal made three attempts to jump a wall before succeeding, and then he saw him creep towards the mouth of a stone drain, slowly and deliberately walk past it to a manure heap. On this he rolled, after which he came back by a series of jumps down wind and disappeared into the drain just as leading hounds crossed the wall sixty yards behind him. The drain, which was usually protected by an iron grating, was fully half a mile long, and led to a threshing-mill pond, and had many side branches; and though large enough to admit a terrier, it was considered by the Duke's people, in whose country it was, too strong to allow of bolting.

A MORNING'S CUBBING

After refreshing man and horse, we started with Jack, who had opportunely turned up, picked up the two missing hounds on the way, and reached kennels at 8 P.M.

Billy emerged from the stables, where he had been watching his mare being dressed over, looking very much injured. He had come home early in the afternoon in the nearest approach to bad temper possible to him, and had received scant sympathy from the household. He was not improved by the remark of a young girl, who innocently inquired if he had had a nice run; and as he had been engaged in chasing his horse for the best part of three hours, he could not reciprocate the smile that flitted over Joanna's face; nor, had he known she had prompted the question to the young lady, could he have immediately forgiven her.

At nine-o'clock dinner, after hearing my tale, he told his.

He declared he had ridden out to stop tail hounds from running a hare that had jumped up from her form in front of their noses, when his mare blundered elbow deep into a soft spot, and shot him over her head. He was up as soon as the mare, but could not catch her. Just as he had cornered the "jade" between two wire fences, "the long-legged besom that she is" hoisted herself over with a buck and made off.

" How and where did you catch her?"

" Caught her in a stackyard two hours later in the middle of the next parish; must have jumped about six fences to get there, and after a wide forward cast round, brought her home; spoiled a hat and lost a spur—made good use of the remaining one, though," he added viciously.

Later on, from the room adjoining the smoke-room, scraps of conversation came drifting. Billy was evidently telling his oft-told tale, and from the tone of his voice, seeking sympathy.

"Are you still thinking of selling 'Quicksilver'?" asked Joan.

"I would willingly have presented her to my dearest foe this morning," he replied. "What's the use of keeping a beast that won't jump when asked, and jumps like a wallaby when not wanted?" Then raising his voice, "I wonder if the Master has written up his journal?"

"Just done so."

"What have you said?"

"Hounds ran a cracker with an old fox from Dodhead cover by Whiterope Moss, Glenlude Linn, and Blaw-wearie Moor to Burnfoot with no help, and without checking, and marked the fox to ground in the Park Mill pond drain—a fourteen-mile point—all up except old Lapwing and one and a half couple of puppies."

"Did you say all the staff was up *at* the drain, or *up* the drain? Because——"

"And lost hounds for a time, and Whipper-in altogether," suggested Joanna.

"I am adding, Second Whip lost his horse, one of his spurs, and part of his temper."

"Never cub unless you're sure of finding cubs," growled Billy.

"Never holler hounds on to an old fox. Good night," was the retort.

A MORNING'S CUBBING

On the smoke-room table next morning we found this draft advertisement:—

For Sale (along with the Forest Hunt Cub Hunters), the Property of W. G. Kerr, Esq.,

Grey Mare "Quicksilver,"
(16 hands, 5 years old)

By "Loadstone" from a "Grey leg" mare.

Undocked, good hunter, a fine free fencer, and fast; very good in a Hill Country.

"And long-tailed, long-pedigreed, long-winded, and long-suffering; warranted not to refuse wire," was added in a feminine hand.

CHAPTER V

FIRST BLOOD

"With silence lead thy many-coloured hounds
In all their beauty's pride. See how they range
Dispersed, how busily this way and that
They cross, examining with curious nose
Each likely haunt."—SOMERVILE.

OUR next venture was more successful. There had been a week of warm dewy nights and sunny days; just the sort of weather to make foxes lie out; and we were at work at daybreak with eighteen and a half couple drawing the open. We had tried through some bracken beds and dry mosses before going on to run hounds through the peat hags on higher ground, when Jack pointed upwards with his whip. Old Peter Amos stood on a hilltop, one arm swinging like a flail in full action, his cap held high on the point of his stick with the other, but quite silent—he knew more than to shout. We climbed up towards him, and seemingly before we were within hailing distance he shouted down the hillside with a voice that would have pierced a snowdrift: "Auld Tweed cam til a deid sett at a heather buss and begood t' girn, an' whan A gaed forrit a muckle foax lap up an' made for the heichts by the Blue Cairn. That was off an' on toonty meenits sin'," he bellowed. We took hounds round to the other side of the Blue Cairn height, and they spread out nicely through some rushy ground feeling for the line, then touching it they darted away and ran heel up wind back over the height.

"Dod, man, that's the back fit they're rinnin'," roared old Peter, who had strode round in surprisingly quick time as the hounds ran right back to the kennel in his "heather buss," then threw up their heads, wheeling round and round. Then he continued in an agony of distress: "Get awa yont, ye rash-heided, donnert deevils; auld Tweed wad made better wark," he added, as I slithered past him blowing the horn, Jack cantering round them to turn them back. In a few minutes we had them put right, and were riding down an easy slope, hounds running along the edge of a long dry moss which ended in a deep watercourse. Crossing this, we had about two miles of rough benty ground, where hounds made away from us, but we got to them again very busy in a large fir plantation. After two or three turns round it, when we cracked our whips and showed ourselves as much as possible, the chorus growing louder and louder, there was a sudden lull, and then Jack's whoop came from the other side. I found him standing by a rabbit burrow, at the mouth of which hounds were baying and tearing the turf and digging like demons.

"Shall we give him any law, sir?" asked Jack.

"Not a bit, sir," replied a perspiring young farmer for me. "There's fer owre mony o' them here-away; they've taen the maist feck o' ma wife's chickens, an' noo they've yokit on the auld clockers."

"Very well; get a paling stob, and we'll soon have him out."

A few minutes' digging disclosed our cub.

"Whoop — whoo-oop — whoo-oo-oop!" screamed Billy.

"Worry—worry—worry— too-too-too —too-too-too —too-too-too-too-oo!" went the horn.

"Must have a pad in memory of first blood."

"Dead, dead, dead; leave it, hounds," said my amateur first whip.

"Very good; but don't lay your whip about you so; don't frighten young hounds; let them break him up outside the cover and eat him."

Jack whipped off the brush and one pad, and holding the carcase up high before tossing it to the hounds, we screamed to our hearts' content.

"All up, sir," said Jack, as Lawless, a rather timid puppy, came in.

We saved a few scraps, pads and tit-bits, for the young hounds, and were coaxing them to taste them, when the boy riding my second horse came with the information that he had seen a fox leave the lower end of the plantation two minutes ago. So, before hounds had recovered their wind, we were cantering round, and soon had the satisfaction of seeing them dash away and settle down to run as if they meant business. A nice wide ring over sound lea heather ground brought us in a quarter of an hour, with one slight check where sheep had crossed the line, to a fair-sized stream, down the bed of which hounds hunted very closely, and where I saw two of the puppies very keen, as they were led to cross and recross the stream. Half a mile lower down were the buildings of a hill farm, a dwelling-house with out-houses behind, standing in an angle formed by the

He faced round at them with wide open jaws.

junction of a smaller stream with this one. A woman and two girls were at the kitchen door gesticulating excitedly.

Billy popped over a fair-sized rail into a sheep-yard, only to pop out again the same way, for the other side was an impossible wall—a most unnecessary performance; but he was always bold with a gallery.

"Please don't scream, Missus," said Billy, as hounds cast all round the outhouses, and the good lady's apron waved, and her stout arm pointed.

"The foax cam by the end o' the hen-hoose an' gaed up the burn."

"Thank you, Missus."

"Pilgrim has it; hark to Pilgrim; huic together, huic!" as the old hound ran up the bed of the burn baying like a bloodhound, the others hastening to him. Up they hunted very prettily to a deep ravine, above which they paused a minute on bare ground, and struck off across the open moor again. They were now running very fast, only a tail hound or two speaking, the leading hounds almost silent, and one or two drawing out from the others.

"There he goes, the poor beggar, he's doomed."

Walking up a bank sparsely covered with hazel-nut bushes was our luckless cub—doubtless brother to the one that met his fate earlier in the morning. He lay down behind a bush, then made a spurt to reach the stream again; but Dexter and Regent getting a view of him, raced up and turned him to Warrior, Pilgrim, and Trojan, who simultaneously grabbed him as he faced round at them with wide-open jaws.

"Here's the brush of a good stout cub for you,

Mr. Grieve," said I to our hen-raising farmer, as that gentleman came panting up.

"Thank ye, sir; that was not his first veesit to my hen-hoose, but it will be his last, the thief. Come roond my way an' I'll gie ye a taste o' butter-milk an' whuskey—a graund drink for a hot mornin'."

"Many thanks, but it's a little out of our way," replied I, glancing at my second whip, who would fain have gone back. "Good morning."

"A satisfactory morning, Master," said Billy, as we sauntered homewards.

"Yes, Bill; all but for one thing. I would have liked it better had hounds found these two foxes entirely by themselves. They hunted them well enough, but they had none of the fun or trouble of hunting *for* them; and if they always have them found for them like this, they may become impatient and careless in drawing."

On that homeward ride, as on many subsequent occasions, we went over minutely every small incident of the morning, discussing the individual performances of each hound; how the old hounds ran in turn at head without jealousy; how one or two of the young ones would dart forward as if to snatch it away from their elders, but when they were in difficulties, how they had to fall back and allow the more experienced to show them how to keep to the line; how this hound was best on the sheep tracks and that across the burnt heather: agreeing that there was a great deal of delight to be had from watching all this, even though the riding part of it was not up to what it is in enclosed country over fences.

Billy devoted a good deal of soliloquy as to what he would have done had he been the fox, and why.

"Now that first beggar, if he had only gone on past Huntly wood, he might have run us out of scent with his twenty minutes' start, instead of trying to push his brother up" (we had decided they were brothers) "and then going and trying to hide. Silly ass! I'd rather have gone till I dropped than stuff my head into a rabbit hole and be half dead with suffocation first, before being dragged out like a condemned criminal. These two cubs showed all the difference between how to die like a soldier, face to the foe, and how to die like a convict."

"Why convict, Bill?"

"Because, don't you see, in his last moments, all his past evil life would come up before him, and he felt so jolly mean-spirited that he didn't care, and convicted himself and hid for very shame."

"After all, I suppose that both the two of them did what they thought to be their duty; and anyhow, they served a purpose. Well, at least, they only obeyed the first instinct of all animals, which is that of self-preservation; and whether their actions were directed by any other motive or not, we cannot tell."

After a pause, the talk took a more serious turn.

Our philosopher remarked: "I suppose we run a certain amount of risk ourselves in galloping over these rough moors; though I take it, and we all take it, as only part of the fun, and we would not ask for less of it."

"Do you know that the Arabs have a proverb—'The horseman's grave is always open'?"

"No; but I rather like it. I don't call myself a

horseman, but when my time comes I'd like—well, what I do funk, really would funk, is a long slow ending, a real bad trouble, or worse still being crippled—ugh! No; anything but that—I'd like it to be short; just the sudden topple into the grave of the Arab."

For many a day did the recollection of that ride home remain in my mind; and, indeed, I rarely think of our "first blood" without recalling every word of our talk as we drank in the delight of that splendid autumn morning.

"I wish we could stop and hunt in these grand hills for all time, eh?"

At first this seemed a strange announcement coming from Billy, whose appreciation of a hunt was in proportion to the number and nature of the fences he met and crossed; who rarely noticed natural scenery; who generally devoted less attention to hounds and hound work than to his own horse's performance, and to that of his friends and rivals; and who hitherto had often spoken slightingly of hunting in the hills.

We had risen gently to the top of some high ground, and were riding through a nick between two hills—a "swire" as it is locally called, with the ground falling away before us—and we looked down upon and across a wide upland valley lit up by an early September sun.

We saw a sea of round-topped hills rolling on every side, the prevailing colour green, but that of an infinite variety of shades, the brown bent grass in the foreground relieved in patches by the gold of the frost-tinted bracken, and in larger stretches by the dull purple of the slow-fading heather; the colouring now contrasting sharply, and now blending harmoniously, as a shaft of the sun rested on it, or a shadow from a drifting cloud dimmed it for a moment. Here and there a spot of grey indicated an out-by shepherd's cottage, with byre and potato ground attached, sometimes poorly protected by a stell of battered Scotch firs, looking in the distance like a bunch of broom bushes, but more often placed in a howe of natural shelter. Black dots were the peats fresh cut and loose stacked, to dry, but not yet led in.

Stone cairns stood silent sentinels on the tops of the more prominent heights; while away to the west blue-grey mists rolled slowly up to the summits and clung to them before joining the clouds floating, like masses of newly-shorn fleece wool, above them.

On either side of the valley, the foot of each long limb stretching down from the higher ground was clothed with a fringe of birk and hazel; the bosoms of the hills were divided by hanging hopes; their shoulders were cleft by sike and cleuch; and their heads were fitted with caps of light veil-like vapour which, from time to time, passed from one to the other.

"Isn't this perfectly heavenly, Billy?"

We gazed spellbound, then glanced at each other, and Billy, in a half whisper, said, "Man, don't speak. O God! these grand green hills!" which was, perhaps, the best expressed prayer he had breathed for years.

We rode in silence for some time, till my companion said, "You don't want me to help you home with the hounds, do you? For I think, if you don't mind, old chap, I'll go round by the Ford." And as I made no reply, he continued, "It's not so far out of the way" (it was a trifle of nine miles or so), "and the day's young yet; and besides, John Elliot has a colt I rather want to see. He's been handling him, and was to back him this week," he continued, talking hurriedly, and looking earnestly across to the other side of the valley.

It was such an unusual custom for Billy to give so many and so minute reasons for his contemplated movements that my curiosity was roused; but without displaying it, I gazed hard into space and waited for more. It came.

"Do you think that bird-skinning, fox-stuffing barber at Midhope Village could give me a decent shave, for I feel rather a nigger?"

"Yes, I think he could; but that's two miles more out of the way."

"Is it so much as that? Then I must saunter on. By-the-by, John said he'd perhaps ride out by the swire on the chance of picking me up."

As soon as he had forced the unwilling grey mare to turn off down the bridle-path and proceed a little way, the saunter was quickened to an easy canter, and before he passed out of sight I saw, not the stout form of John Elliot, but a slim figure in a skirt, on a white pony, appearing from the opposite direction. The two converged, met, and then rode away together through the shining hills.

CHAPTER VI

GETTING TO WORK

> " *When autumn is flaunting her banner of pride*
> *For glory that summer has fled,*
> *Arrayed in the robes of his royalty, dyed*
> *In tawny and orange and red;*
> *When the oak is yet rife with the vigour of life*
> *Tho' his acorns are dropping below,*
> *Thro' bramble and brake shall the echoes awake*
> *To the ring of a clear 'Tally-ho!'*"
>
> —WHYTE-MELVILLE.

ONE of the closing days of September saw us, about 6 A.M., turn our horses' heads away from our summer quarters and point towards the lower country, to take possession of the kennels made ready for us in the so-called Forest country proper, to make acquaintance with the people and the country, and to begin the serious business of regular hunting.

Not without regret did we leave behind the scene of our first efforts and get off the moorland track on to macadamised roads, between hedgerows, through cultivated land.

About half-way, to our anxiety, we heard hounds in chase in the distance, and realised we were in danger of joining in with the "Duke's." Trotting back for half a mile, we held hounds up till the cry ceased.

We would fain have shut our own hounds up and

followed, but we were encumbered with headstalls, and couples, and muzzles, and small stable impedimenta, so we refrained, and moved cautiously forward. No hounds broke away, but we shortly afterwards missed two terriers. The keen little creatures had made off and followed the fun, coupled together, till they were caught hung up on a wire fence quite exhausted and showing marks of a severe battle.

We made out the rest of the journey without further incident, and found all in readiness for us. Hounds signalised their entry into their new quarters by bursting open an unbolted door into the feeding-house, while Tom was attending to his horse, and feeding themselves.

The preparations for our reception included, besides a well-stocked larder, an old beef horse which, from the size and shape of one of his hind-legs, we named "Bedpost." He was afflicted with grease, and was fond of leaning up against a support and scratching the affected leg with his sound one.

On the way to the kennels next morning we found that old "Bedpost" had, during the night, been supporting himself against a rail fence surrounding the tennis lawn. He had begun at one end, and carrying away a rood at a time, had worked his way along, levelling the whole to the ground. He then got his rump comfortably wedged against an old arbour, which, though he did not raze, he canted considerably off the straight. That day he was turned into the cowfield, which was surrounded by a strong iron fence, in which apparently secure barrier he found a weak spot; for about 3 A.M. I was wakened by a stamping noise outside the front door, continued at regular

Old "Bedpost" scratching the affected leg.

intervals, and kept up so long that I went down. There I found old "Bedpost" leaning on the iron railing at the foot of the stone steps, indulging in his practice of scratching his big leg. The poor beast was soon afterwards converted into soup.

Hounds were received with symptoms of great enthusiasm by all dwellers in the Forest country; not only by those who followed them, but by many who never had been, and could never hope to be, out with them. During the early days of cubbing in the first season, many indications were shown of a strong interest in the hunt, and a keen appreciation of the sport.

An old farmer occupying land adjoining the kennels never missed seeing hounds go out in the morning; no matter how early they left the kennels, old Wight was at his gate to see us pass; and though rather a solemn-looking individual at ordinary times, he always had a wide grin to give us and a salute much more marked and ceremonious than on other occasions. A hand raised half-way up to his hat and a sort of backward jerk of his head was his market-day recognition; but a low bow and a downward sweep of his hat was always given to the hounds. He was equally anxious for our safe return; and if he had not seen us come in before dark, he used to make his wife and son take turns to watch and listen. The latter, one night, got tired of his cold vigil, and reported our return to his father, who, unfortunately for Tom's veracity, heard the horn sounding to acquaint the stablemen of our approach an hour later. The old man suspecting Tom's error, asked me at what hour we got back, and on being told 7.30, he said, "An' Tammas had ye hame an oor suner, the leein' thief; he's a guid pleughman, but he wad never dae for a hunter, him."

The old man used to supply the stable with straw and oats, and was with difficulty coaxed into the house one day to get a settlement of his account for provender. Only the bribe of a promised dram, and the assurance that there were no women-folk about, overcame his shyness and reluctance; but once in, the trouble was to get him to leave. At parting he said: "It wad been a positeeve calamity if ye hadna come forrit to cairry on the hoonds. I think ye'll dae; aye, I think ye'll dae. I wasna share aboot ye at first, I thocht ye was owre prood."

The same old gentleman was not without a sense of humour. Meeting him one market day, he accosted me as follows:—

"A saw a graun fox hunt last week. The fox cam doon the furr juist twae feerins aff whaur Tam was plewin', an' the whole o' the hoonds sune efter, doon the verra same furr, gein' mooth graund, a bonnie sicht a' thegither, fox an' hoonds, an' a'; but," with a dig in my ribs, "nae riders, nae riders."

His farm was intersected, as much of the country is, by a long deep glen, with only one or two crossing-places; and if the chase leads over such a place, unless you hit upon a crossing it is often a case of "nae riders."

The hill men were especially keen, real sportsmen, with an inborn love of horse and hound, and an intimate knowledge of the science and craft of hunting. They knew the likely lie of a fox in all weathers, and his probable line when hunted, and were most appreciative of hound work, and quick to observe it.

GETTING TO WORK

Good stockmen and breeders, most of them had the trained eye of the natural judge of form, and could tell at a glance a true-shaped horse. They generally possessed a good one or two of their own breeding, and, while careful to ease them when occasion demanded, got the most possible out of them when required.

I used to admire the way they slipped off their horse, then threw the reins over his head, and ran at top speed down the steepest hillside, the sensible beast neither hanging back nor rushing on, but adjusting his pace to that of his master, and following like a trained dog, the pair arriving at the bottom and being away again together before a less active and less practised man had made up his mind whether to get down and lead or not.

It was a pretty sight to see them lift their terrier on to the saddle in front of them, as they often did, by getting him on to the top side of the slope, taking a foot out of their stirrup, and stretching it out towards him. The eager little beggar would half jump, half scramble till he was grabbed hold of and planted down on the thigh of his master, who would then canter off in no way inconvenienced by his awkward burden.

The way they get over their own country, without getting *in*, is remarkable, for much of it is almost unrideable, except to the man and horse who know how to do it. It is their pride to boast they have hunted a whole season, or several seasons, as may be the case, and without ever having been "laired." Many a good chase have I enjoyed assisted by the observations and example of one or other of these hard hill lads.

Not one whit behind their masters in keenness and in fondness of fox-hunting are the hill shepherds. From their point of vantage on a hilltop, behind a stone cairn perhaps, they often see more of the incidents of the chase than a regular follower. With an eye like a hawk's, they can view a fox as soon as ever he stirs a mile off. They can pick him up as he crawls along the loose stones of the slithers on a bare hillside, as he creeps the bottom of a sheep drain, or as he slinks through the bracken beds, taking advantage of the formation and colour of every bit of ground to conceal himself till he has selected his point; and then they can mark him streaking away like a yellow flash to the heights; and even long after he is beyond their sight, they see his course by the movement of the sheep, and the swooping of the curlews and the plovers.

Their delight is to see the hounds run the line out of sight and hearing, and to wait and watch for them coming back again with a tired fox close before them.

Their dogs are shut up at home on hunting days, and they rarely shout, but communicate their intelligence by waving their handkerchiefs on the end of a stick.

I remember a young lad running the best part of two miles to tell me my hunted fox had lain down on a heap of loose stones, and that hounds were running the line of one that had been disturbed by the cry, and had slunk away before we had come into sight.

But all over the same interest existed. The farm labourers and roadmen were alike pleased to see

GETTING TO WORK

hounds, and were delighted to report any incident they had observed.

They seldom spoke of the fox as such by his name. An old road-mender, bent double with rheumatism and leaning on two sticks, said one day: "Oo had a veesit frae yin o' yer freen's last nicht, sir. He liftit twae duicks till us. The wife's kinda compleenin', but A'm no sayin' a word masel." Or: "A saw *him* the nicht afore last i' the grey derk; he *was* a yalla yin! eh, he was a muckle yalla yin! no' the little reed yin A tell't ye o' afore."

Great was the disappointment of the folk if a fox was not found on their own farm.

"Hae ye no raised him yet, sir?" said a jolly-looking farm steward, as I was blowing hounds out after a blank draw.

"Not yet, Sandy."

"Did ye try Braeside whin, an' no raise him there?"

"No, Sandy."

"Dod, that bates a', an' me saw twae there the other Sunday. A dander oot maist every Sunday efternuin to see if A can see him."

A good type of hill farmer was Tom Telfer, by his own inclination and desire, endorsed by common consent and unanimous selection, official First Whip to the Hunt. Born and brought up in the hills, he knew every yard of ground on both sides of the Border line in a twenty-mile radius from home, had early developed a liking for field sports, and soon acquired a faculty for crossing a rough country that was remarkable even in a community of hard riders. He was always well mounted; but, indeed, whatever he rode had got to go where and how he wanted, and whether it liked it or not, although it generally seemed to like it. His horses never pulled or fought with him. He had one infallible cure for a rash or impetuous one. "The first time out let the beggar stretch his neck well and tire him out proper, he'll never forget it or want to pull again." It was a treat to see him on a young or half-broken horse, for before the end of the day he had him with the manners of an old one.

But where he shone most was in a long fast chase over a difficult country. He was generally seen sailing away in front with the greatest apparent ease, picking his place in the fences, riding straight at them, and turning away from nothing, when suddenly we would see him shoot out right or left and gallop for all he was worth. He had seen leading hounds swing round one way or the other, and quick as thought he was cutting across to get to them. Of course, he at one time took many falls, but being light, wiry, and supple, he thought little of them.

Having whipped in to my predecessor for six years intermittently since the foundation of the pack, he was no tyro, and knew the game well. Some laughable occurrences had taken place in the embryonic days before the Hunt had developed and blossomed into the stage of advertising.

It is told of him that he had a heated altercation with the huntsman on the occasion of the two worthies donning pink for the first time. What made the scene all the more ludicrous was, that the huntsman, to complete his costume, had to wear a top-hat, his cap not having come forward, and his bowler being battered and green with age. A gale of wind made the hounds, hurriedly snatched together from the drafts of three or four kennels, wild and unhandy after being off work for a fortnight during an early frost. They had been half coaxed, half threatened, into a plantation which generally held a fox, and immediately ran riot, for unfortunately the wood was full of hares, and a good deal of rating had been heard, more professional than amateur. Tom Telfer had seen a fox leave, and galloped round to the huntsman, choking with excitement.

"What the—why the—where the deuce are you? Blow your horn, man, blow, the fox is away!"

Resenting being told in this fashion, the huntsman retaliated: "Crack your whip, man, crack!"

"Man alive! you blow your horn!"

"Snakes alive! you crack your whip!"

This was the beginning of the colloquy, and then Tom roared to his superior: "It's your business to gallop on and blow in front of the hounds to get them out!"

"It's your place to go back behind hounds and crack them out to me!"

"Blow, blow, you blockhead, blow!"

"Now, Tom, if you're going to sit there and sing hymns to me we'll never get on. Crack! crack! you crazy critter, crack! Which way did you say he had gone?"

But meanwhile two fast, jealous, and mute hounds—Driver and Duster—had slipped away, not unperceived by Tom Telfer, who straightway went after them like a sky rocket, and the rest of the day was spent in following the somewhat mixed line of scent of the fox, Tom Telfer, and one couple of hounds, which caused the pack, and consequently the field, to string out considerably. When, as the dusk was drawing in, huntsman and whip next met —it was at a cavernous-looking earth among the peat hags on the top of Windburgh—there were no listeners within earshot to hear what were the complimentary words that passed between them.

One of the keenest of the keen was Andrew Waugh, a contracting mason, who did a fair amount of trade for most of the country houses round, building and renewing farm offices, and such work. One of his specialties was kitchen ranges and ovens, and the cure of smoky chimneys. One day, after taking down a kitchen range, and being on the house-top repairing a chimney-can, he spied hounds trotting off to draw a very likely plantation. He promptly slid down the ladder, and dragging his pony from its feed of corn, joined in with his working apron on, and with all the ardour of a school-boy released from school. Needless to say, his contract knew him no more that day, and the mansion had to cook its dinner on the scullery stove till the pony, cut during that day's hunt, had sufficiently recovered to carry its master to his job.

My introduction to him was on an Abbotvale day, when hounds were in full cry with a very blown cub brought in from the hills which they had been running hard, with short respite, for half-an-hour, and which they were driving from one clump of shrubbery to another, till he lay down and momentarily baffled them. I remember being particularly anxious that

GETTING TO WORK 63

there should be no noise, and that hounds should work up to him, and push him up. Suddenly there rose yells and shouts—"Yonder he is; he's intae the gairden; shut the door an' they'll hev 'im," and a group of pedestrian onlookers swept *en masse* to the garden door as hounds poured through it. At the head of this detachment rode an old man, wildly waving his cap, and spurring his rough horse with his one spur, attached, to be more effective, upside down. His face was beaming with delight, and he thundered down a gravel path to the bottom of the garden just in time to see the wretched fox scramble over the high upright picket fence in front of a yelling pack. On he clattered out at the avenue gate, up to the hounds, through them, and away in front of them. A high stiff gate across a narrow lane will surely check him; not a bit; for flailing his willing horse he rushed it, and with a terrible rattle landed clear on the other side, just as hounds turned suddenly back in pursuit of the doubling fox.

A minute or two later they were in full chorus through the policies again, our friend at the head of affairs. I thought it was time to interfere, so riding up, I began, "Hold hard; hold hard, please. Hi there, will you hold hard, please?" Then getting alongside I, nearly choking with rage, said, "Can't you hear hounds are *behind* you?"

"He hears nothing, sir," explained Jack. "He's stone deaf."

The honest fellow turned round and showed a face glowing with enjoyment and triumph, and as I pulled the Omega mare back he shouted, "They were terrible near him at the gairden fit. Come on, sir," and gesticulating as if inviting me to a trial of speed. When the fox was killed behind us, and a pad was presented to this fearless old fellow, he said, "A wadna wonder if ma beast grows inta a hunter yet; an' what a graund hunt we've hed; an' a nice bit loup that neabody taen bit me an' the Maister."

This was my first acquaintance with this grand old sportsman.

On the way home we passed by the side of the road a spring cart with a wheel in the ditch, and harness thrown down or scattered about anyhow.

"Has there been an accident?" said some one.

"Oh no," was the explanation, "this is old Andrew. He was driving away to mend the roofs at Netherhouses when he got sight of hounds, and thereupon converted his carriage horse into a hunter."

It was after about ten days' experience of these first days that Billy said to me: "I say, Master, if anything was to happen to you (or to me) there'ud be no lack of material for a huntsman. The way some of these boys get to hounds and know what they are doing is astonishing—a bit too noisy though, some of them."

"Perhaps, Bill, but it's only their keenness, and they know not to do it when hounds are on their noses and casting round to recover a line."

CHAPTER VII

A DAY WITH THE DUKE

"Pleasure that the most enchants us
Seems the soonest done;
What is life, with all it grants us,
But a hunting run!"—WHYTE-MELVILLE.

IT had been arranged that we should take a day with the Duke's hounds, and a special effort was being made by every one of the house party to put in a creditable appearance, both as to horse and kit. I was unable to go, having business to attend to at home; but was mounting Captain Richards, an old friend and fine horseman, on my best; and our numbers were increased by a lady, Miss Anstruther, and a gallant soldier, Major Thurston, who had come to hunt and stay, bringing their own horses. Both were very good in their own way, but a little jealous. Billy, Florence Elliot, and a schoolboy completed the party.

Breakfast was to be half-an-hour earlier than usual, and Billy and Miss Florence were a quarter of an hour late, owing to the extra time each had devoted in the morning-room to the adjusting of the other's scarf, which seemed to be models of neatness and whiteness; though the young lady's required more protracted manipulation from the deft fingers of the gentleman than appeared requisite.

"How's my stock, Mr. Kerr?" she had asked.

After the most searching examination, the verdict was—"Beautifully folded, but the pin is a *trifle* high, and might be a *leetle* more sloped. May I put it right for you?" and so on.

This operation had been witnessed through the open window by Bobby, to his great joy, and he stored up what he had seen and heard for further use.

"Aunt Jane is late," said Joanna from behind the urn, as the tramp of horses' feet was heard on the gravel.

"I don't think Aunt Jane will appear till she knows I am well away," exclaimed Captain Richards. "I fear I am the innocent cause of her absence," he went on. "I met her as I was coming along the passage with my white apron on, and I believe she thought it was another sort of garment, and that I was on my way to the bath-room, for in spite of my most agreeable smiles and greeting, she cut me dead and ran off with half-suppressed sobs."

The first incident of note, after the cavalcade started, was that Bobby's Shetland pony made a rush to a watering-trough by the roadside, and plunging his muzzle in over the nostrils, drank deep and long. His rider tugged, and flogged, and kicked, and Captain Richards flicked clouds of dust out of his shaggy coat with his whip, all to no purpose, until his thirst was slaked.

"I told Batters to keep the water off him last night," said Bobby. "Never mind, I don't need to draw up my girths now; they're quite tight enough."

Bobby bolted *underneath* it at the risk of being scraped off.

A DAY WITH THE DUKE

They came home in the evening in detachments. Bobby was an easy first, bringing in his still panting pony with one shoe, and bearing the incredible intelligence that he had stopped most of the field. Whether he was more proud of this last accomplishment or of losing three shoes it is not easy to decide. The main body returning later confirmed the news. The facts were, that a tall untrimmed hedge had temporarily checked part of the field, who were craning and looking for a weak outlet, and Lord Charles' horse had shied off the formidable obstacle, when Bobby spied a gap with a long tree or spar fixed across it, about four feet six inches from the ground, and crouching along the side of his $11\frac{1}{2}$-hand hunter, had bolted *underneath* it at the risk of being scraped off. It is only fair to say that Lord Charles, following him, flew the uninviting leap without a fault.

Loud were the praises of the hounds, the huntsman, and the country by all gathered round the tea-table, and the field's gallantry was specially sung by Miss Florence.

On the last point Billy was more silent than was his wont. It transpired that during a very fast scurry in the afternoon, Billy had not been as much in evidence as usual.

But to Master Bobby belonged the honours of the day. He had ridden through the hounds, and was chatting quite at his ease with the huntsman, when the Duke rode up. Just before moving off, His Grace had asked who the schoolboy was in the cricket cap, and Bobby was duly presented. He was eating his sandwiches at the moment, or rather sharing them with an old hound who was hiding behind his pony, but snatched off his cap in salutation, which, as he could not replace, he crammed into his pocket, and then extended a very rough woolly and not overclean gloved hand in the Duke's direction. The sixteen-hand hunter edged away from the rough doormat of a pony; but Bobby was not to be baffled, and urged his mount alongside, the Duke good-naturedly bending forward and nearly overbalancing himself as he stretched out his arm to the persistent boy. Still the nervous horse shied back and snorted.

"So ho, don't be afraid, old man," said Bobby, as he succeeded in obtaining a firm grasp of the hand, and wrung it with the fervour of an old comrade, and to an extent that nearly pulled the noble Master out of his saddle.

I have always experienced some difficulty in obtaining a clear and connected account of a day's hunting from those engaged in it—a difficulty amounting, at times, to despair. If the questioned party belongs to the gentle sex, the trouble is most acute, and there is only slight hope of collecting a coherent report, especially if there should happen to be present another fair participator in the day's proceedings all too eager to recount her experiences.

I am frequently forcibly reminded of the saying of an old huntsman on this point, who was very shrewd and observant, and who had a very terse and direct way of putting things. It was as follows: "The merit of a run greatly depends upon the position held in it by the narrator." Bearing this in mind, I looked forward with something more

A DAY WITH THE DUKE

than ordinary interest to the versions I was to hear, knowing they would be varied. The ladies had already thrashed out every minute of the day at the tea-table, in their bed-rooms, and at dinner, but were delighted to be invited into the smoke-room at ten o'clock for a further palaver.

My initial question of where the fox was found was completely ignored, and the line of talk taken and followed consisted mostly of interjections as to what each had seen the other do.

"Did you have a *very* awkward post and rail in a corner?"

"Did you see me jump the drop?"

"How did my mare do the double?"

"Didn't Mrs. Black's horse peck badly there?"

These were questions fired off by Miss Anstruther to Florence with such startling rapidity as almost to preclude reply.

"Where was the double?" I ventured to ask.

"Oh, just after we crossed a muddy lane, and through a gate, along a grass field, over a horrid little trappy fence into a sticky plough, not far from the donkey," was the enlightening reply, reeled off, amid laughter, without a pause, by the eager lady.

This one feature of the donkey seemed to be prominent in the recollection of all, and served as a basis comparative for time and locality.

It seemed hounds had checked for a minute or two behind some farm buildings, and on recovering the line and throwing their tongues, a donkey in an orchard adjoining had lifted up his voice and brayed loudly.

So it was, "Captain Stone fell before the donkey."

"I didn't have my lunch till after the donkey." And, "The double was just about the same time as the donkey."

"But where was the tremendous double?" again I asked, while various items of information, relevant or otherwise, were rapidly volunteered. "Was it in the afternoon, or in the morning hunt?"

"The afternoon, I think," replied Miss Anstruther; "at least, Lord Charles had his second horse, and he and Major Thurston were at it first, and I came next, the first woman, except that Mrs. Black, who had it lower down at a *much* easier place, Mr. Kerr told me. I saw her in trouble soon after, and I don't think she can go much without a pilot. Yes it was just about the donkey."

Florence, who had been waiting for an opportunity, now chimed in, "It was on the line between Cotley and Brownmoor, and on old Moffat's farm," she said triumphantly, after a whispered consultation with Billy, who may have prompted her. Miss Florence had followed hounds on a pony as a schoolgirl; but this was only her second season on a grown horse. She was quite inexperienced in a crowd, and a little over-anxious not to be in the way; but had a decided knack of getting along without being conspicuous or seeming to be in a hurry. She had a good eye for a country, and an unfailing memory; a wrong turn once taken was always remembered and never again repeated. She never "coffee-housed," and at a check always stood still outside the crowd, watching, so usually got a good start. Her great desire was to become a thorough sportswoman, to learn the country well, to get to hounds, to know and see what they were doing, and to save her horse as much as possible. All she knew she had learnt with the Forest fox-hounds, and I was distinctly disappointed to hear that though she had held her own well in the morning, she had not been quite " in it " in the afternoon.

"It was a real nice day's sport, my Uncle," she said. " Hounds did not get a good start from Cotley gorse. They hunted the best part of two hours, and were kept busy all the time; it was a ringing hunt, but they took us over some nice country; never fast, but always kept moving on. They ran by Catshawhill, Friarshaw Moor, and the Fans, and crossed the river twice, at the Lowlynn ford and again higher up. Anyhow, 'Nugget' and I had enough to do, and I was not sorry when they ran into the fox at Sandymill, five miles from where they found him."

The gallant Major must be catalogued in the class along with those who hunt to ride. An undeniably fine horseman, with good nerve and judgment, he was generally well mounted, and prominently in front. But he was handicapped with short sight that prevented him from seeing hounds cutting out the work in a close country, and with shorter temper that came to the front when he lost his place and fell back. In fact, he liked to be first or nowhere. I anticipated his reply to my " Now, Major Thurston ? "

" Well, it was very slow in the mornin', with time to pick your place twice over, and lots of time to get out of the way of the boys and girls. Not much leppin'; a nice fence or two now and again, but nothin' that a pony couldn't jump, and hounds kept checkin', and ringin', and dwellin'."

"Not much 'dwell' from Harestanes, Major," put in Richards.

"No, it was certainly better in the afternoon; a fastish ten minutes over a fairish country that took some doin'; if they had only gone on there wouldn't have been many in it."

"Fastish!" screamed several voices; "it's four miles on the map, and I swear we did not take more than fifteen minutes to it. Why, it's racing. It's 'Grand National' form."

"I would sum it up," persisted the Major, "by saying it was an indifferent day, relieved by a smart dash in the afternoon."

"Well, Master," said Richards, "I call it a very first-rate day's sport" (he had ridden in many point to point races, and between the flags). "Hounds ran quite fast enough over a stiffish enclosed country, with a twisting fox headed back once or twice, and on an uncertain scent. They stuck well to the line, and put in some very pretty work. The huntsman was very patient and persevering; let them alone at the critical time, and encouraged them at the right moment; and worked hard all through the show sport. As to the afternoon gallop, you wanted a steeplechase horse to be near it, and, thanks to you, I had one."

Billy's chief contribution to the discussion was grunted out between clouds of smoke from his pipe: "Some of these fellows ride big bang blood horses up to two stone over their weight, and know the country like their pockets;" and added, "I wasn't in the afternoon spurt."

Bobby's shrill treble now piped up from a dark corner of the sofa, where he had been sleeping unnoticed: "The old Duke's a brick, but Freddy Elliot's a prig. He does swagger so about a brush he's got at home, some poor cub's likely, or a mangy vixen's," he continued, as an afterthought. "By-the-bye, Mr. Kerr, it was jolly decent of you to wait and girth up cousin Florence, and tie her tie, as I saw you doing in the stackyard at Harestanes, just as the hounds were going away."

This interjection threw some light on Billy's absence from the afternoon spurt.

"Be off to bed with you, you young whelp," said Billy, taking him by the shoulder and hustling him out of the room.

After the ladies had retired, the talk was prolonged till past midnight. It sometimes passed away temporarily from horses and hounds, but always drifted back to this oft-travelled channel, and from all sides reminiscences came ready and rife. The Duke's huntsman came in for a full share of the discussion.

"How did you like him?" said I to Captain Richards.

"I think it would be well worth riding fifty miles on a rough horse if only to have a look at him, the way he sits his horse, and the way he winds his scarf round his neck. He's a hard-bitten purpose-like old man; looks a workman and a bit of a character too."

"He's all that," came from several voices; and then some recollections of him were given.

"I remember," said the Major, "coming upon him standing at the edge of the big wood at Bailliestane on a very windy day, when, for the time being, we were out of sight and hearing of hounds. He was watching a fox going right away, well out across a good country, before he touched his horn. Hounds soon came streaming out, and apparently ran the line so far, then turned at right angles back towards the wood. He blew till he was purple; then laying down the horn, said, 'Look at that. What in wonder is taking them down there? Isn't that most *excruciating?*'

"Again, when hounds had divided for the moment, and we were hesitating which to follow, and an ardent young sportsman rode up to him saying, 'There are some hounds on.' 'I'm aware of that, sir; but don't you hear the major portion of the pack running back like *distraction?*'"

On another occasion, a wild stormy day in the end of March, we had drawn a large tract of country blank till late in the afternoon, when we found a fox in a long strip of plantation, from end to end of which and then across some fields to another plantation, hounds ran. It was then found to be a vixen they were running, so they were stopped, not without some difficulty. Meanwhile one or two of the field had viewed, or thought they had viewed, a dog fox away from some scattered whin bushes outside the first strip, and the news spread. Hounds had crossed the supposed line and had not indicated it. Then one after another, down to the youngest, no less than three members of the Ducal family came to the huntsman with the intelligence.

"You know a fox went away from the end of the strip when hounds were running the other," said No. 1.

"Indeed, my lud?"

Now No. 2 waiting his opportunity, "Perhaps you didn't hear that a fox went away, and it——"

"Did he, my lud?"

Lastly No. 3, a schoolboy full of importance, bustled up, "I say, I don't suppose you heard" (our friend was fairly tired of *hearing* by this time) "that a fox, a dog fox too, went away, &c. Oh yes, there's no doubt about it, for Mr. A. saw him, and some others saw him."

"Did they, indeed, my lud? *Privileged persons!*"

A bold rider himself, he was merciless to a shirker or a funker. A high strong rail had stopped a bevy of these one day, till one enterprising spirit charged and broke the top rail. A confirmed funker asked, "Who is the culprit?"

"What do you say?" said the huntsman.

"Who is the malefactor?"

"Surely you mean, who is the benefactor."

One time, in a crowd of over-anxious horsemen, who had headed a not very adventurous fox back, as he turned his horse round, hemmed in for the moment, he whispered to me, "There's nothing more *injurious* to fox-hunting than mad haste. Where is the sense of pressing on when the fox is back?"

On these lines conversation flowed on till the small hours.

CHAPTER VIII

A TERRIER TALK

*"They may wind him and find him and hustle him round,
They may race him and chase him and put him to ground,
But here in the heart of the hill countree
How seldom they'd eat him without help from me!"*
—"SCAMP."

"IF you wish to find Bill you had better look the stables," had often been said to me by the Lady President of the establishment; and the same reliable person now stated that she had that morning instructed the servant to say to a Lady Collector who had called at the door, that if she wished to find the Master she had better look the kennels. "Be sure you say the fox-hound kennels, Parker!" was added as an afterthought, to be more impressive, and possibly in hope of inspiring terror.

The Lady Collector, who was described as of a patient and persistent type, did not try for me in the kennels; at least her advent was not reported, although she had been seen in the vicinity.

I did not draw the stables blank for Bill, whom I found standing behind the grey mare's stall talking so earnestly and confidentially to Batters that my approach on the straw was not heard, and I caught the latter muttering: "Weel, sir, ye'll mebbe tak the rue if ye dinna folla ma advice an' get quitten o'—" The remainder was merged in a prolonged "Hiss-s-s-ss!"

"I wonder if you would ever tire of talking horse, Bill?"

"Don't know. Perhaps not until you tired of talking hounds and hunting, or got bored with listening to my drivel, eh?"

As this was the third day of a frost, and as it looked like lasting, we agreed that the latter question might be put to the test, and that in the evening we would try it.

It may have been the enforced idleness that put mischief into my companion's head, and he took advantage of a rare opportunity of playing a practical joke upon his hostess. He had seen or heard of the Lady Collector, and had obtained a minute description of her attire, which was something between that of the Salvation Army and a hospital nurse. He was at great pains to collect sundry articles, which he deposited in a scattered heap by the side of the path leading to the garden. They included half of a well-chewed golosh, pieces of an old straw poke bonnet, shreds of blue serge, red ribbon, whalebone stays, &c. After some hesitation he added a rib or two and the thigh-bone of an old horse; but mercifully these had been removed by old Lapwing, who at that time was allowed her liberty for the benefit of her health. He enticed his "Grandma," as he often called her, out for a walk, and suddenly remarked in a very solemn tone of voice as they neared the heap, "O Granny, look what I found on the floor of the kennels a little while ago!"

For two seconds, but two seconds only, did the terrified lady blanch and tremble; and had not Billy himself exhibited a sudden change from a triumphant attitude to one of dismay at the effect of his ruse, the results might have been more decided.

Then, "Oh! you horror!" screamed Joanna, "you don't for a moment imagine I am taken in by your horrid trick? You don't suppose I thought there had been an accident? I confess that I thought at first they might have torn her cloak perhaps."

"I believe you thought they had eaten her, Granny."

"Poof! not a bit!" Then, as her colour returned, "Tell me exactly what did happen, and don't ever try such a trick again."

"Well now, Gran'ma," said the penitent Bill, "I'll tell you what I'll do. If the lady comes round here again to-morrow, as she said she'd do, I'll give my subscription *vice* the Master."

And he was as good as his word, and was mulcted of ten shillings for the S.P.C.A.

Billy was a good talker, and he was also, what made him so chummable, a good listener; and he was now in his best listening mood. He began the evening by singing the praises of the Border terriers, a comparatively modern breed, very sharp and game, but one of which I had little actual experience.

"Then what sort do you like best?" said he.

"You want for this country a terrier that can run with hounds, or, better still, that can follow up and run behind hounds—the sort that hunts a cover or darts away on a fox's line is useless. If he can be taught and trained to keep back with the second horseman so much the better. You want one that won't tire, but is forward to come up handy when he's wanted, and will 'go in' right up to the fox below ground and will speak to him before he tries to tackle him. Jock here is great at this; he goes in like a bolt from a bow, and squeezes right up to the beggar without loss of time, and gives him notice to quit. If he can't get right up to him he will lie up and bark till he is hoarse, and this always lets one know where he is, and saves time if digging is required. He has the valuable habit of coming out then, and waiting and watching to see if his orders are going to be obeyed, for nothing makes a fox more likely and more anxious to bolt, if he has anything left in him at all, than, after having been well sworn at, to find his attacking enemy retire in silence. Then, if his orders are not obeyed, Jock goes in again with even more determination. How he manages I don't know. I think he only says and looks, 'Cut along out of this or I'll murder you!' Anyhow, his threats are nearly always promptly acted on, and the fox, feeling far safer above ground though pursued by the pack, than being niggled at and tormented by a little demon in the darkness below ground, once more faces the daylight and often gives a good chase, thanks to dauntless little Jock."

"Yes," said Bill, "I think it's the most tremendous piece of pluck ever exhibited or possible to dream of. Think of it. To crawl up a long pitch dark tight hole leading into the earth's bowels, and often filled with ice-cold water, and to boldly attack his unseen foe; a foe his equal in weight, possibly superior in power of punishment, equally savage, and most probably occupying a better position for repelling attack than he does. 'Pon my word, it's equal to a man stalking a wounded tiger on foot! How's he bred? And which do you consider the best kind of breed?"

"Jock came from a Yorkshire Hunt kennel, and is three parts smooth fox and one part bull terrier. I don't think the breed matters much, so long as the *game* is there. I like the first cross between the rough and smooth fox, and a medium size and weight. Coat is all-important; the smooth coats are too thin, and the all rough when thoroughly wetted through don't dry. This cross often produces a thick close coat like a doormat, which is the best of all. And you must have them a little on the leg, not only for running, but to keep them off the slush and wet; length of leg don't matter so long as they are not too thick round the heart."

"How long has he been below ground at a stretch?"

"Once, at Timpendean Castle breeding earth, he got in on Saturday afternoon, and we dug him out on Monday, forty-five hours later. He was fairly wedged in like a wad in a cartridge case, and, though a bit hoarse and feeble in his bark, quite comfortable and unpunished. He was lying on his side, his fore-legs pushed back like a seal's flappers, trying to push himself on with his hind-legs."

"My word!" was the commentary: "any more?"

"Well, most of them have been in for about

twenty-four hours, and Mack there was forty-two hours below and very nearly died of suffocation. He went in with a hunted fox at the large earth at Howden Burn, opposite Wild-Cat Gate, and though we waited till after dark hearing the fighting and struggling shifting from one end to the other, the fox would not bolt, so we left them. On Sunday the keeper reported he could occasionally hear some deep growling; and though some digging was done, the only effect was to drive them deeper in. Mack is too silent and very savage; and all Monday morning we dug. It was one of those dangerous earths in a stratum of fine dry yellow sand, where sides and roof are apt to tumble in and block up the whole passage. About one o'clock we located a faint thumping and drove a shaft down to it, and came right upon the fox. He was only recently dead, not stiff, and still quite warm, and deeply bitten all round the neck. The terrier was lying facing him, completely exhausted and badly punished. He got dreadfully cold when taken out, and shivered so that he could not lap the warm milk we had brought, and we had to feed him. After this, and a shake, and a roll, he so far recovered as to walk home. I remember the fox, a fine old dog, weighed $19\frac{1}{2}$ lbs., and the terrier only 17 lbs."

"I suppose they are nearly always 'in grips' when you get at them?"

"Not always. For sometimes the fox gets so far back, or into some side tunnel, where the terrier can't get at him, that he is apt to come away if he thinks he is being left alone."

"What is the best grip when the jaws are locked?"

"Well, it is not easy to say. The terrier in most cases has the fox by the nose, but this of course leaves the fox's under jaw free to bite. This, I fancy, is what every inexperienced terrier does, and why he gets so punished himself in the lower jaw. Of course, the most killing grip is when the terrier gets nose and lower jaw together, and this is what an old experienced dog will fight for. But once pinned, I don't think a fox can punish much; when he does the mischief is when he is free and can give those long slashing cuts at his attacker."

"Do you like one, or two, out?"

"Only one, unless they are coupled together; for, if loose, they are very apt to get into the same earth or drain. No. 1 is looking in or sniffing at the entrance; No. 2 comes up, and rather than let him in, No. 1 proceeds to explore, though he has already determined there is no fox there. No. 2 follows up till his progress is arrested by No. 1, and out of pure devilment he bites him if they are not good friends, and a battle starts. If they *are* good friends, No. 2 will start to scrape and dig, and is apt to throw the earth back and so stop egress. I had two gallant little two-season terriers suffocated in this way."

"Jock seems more scarred than before. Have you been taking him out oftener than usual lately?"

"Jocky comes out *when*, and as often as, he pleases. Often do we want to leave him in when his old face is barely healed from wounds of the previous week, and have shut him up, but it is useless; he will eat, climb, or burst his way out of any enclosure. Once he climbed over a nine foot wire netting yard turned over at the top.

"Scurry" lying curled up beside him growling savagely.

Another time he ate through the thick door of a stable and burst through a pane of glass; and once he climbed up through the chimney of the boiling-house, and joined hounds."

"Well done, Jock. The only thing that would hold him would be a fire and burglar proof safe! Which is the gamest terrier you've ever known, Master?"

"Well! Jock, Mack, Scamp, and Scurry, I put in that order; but with very little difference between them. Scurry once bolted a fox from a three hundred yard long stone conduit only to drive him into another one running underneath the main Hawick road. This was in a hollow, but the road had been mounded up four or five feet, and the tackling took place right under the centre of the road, and we had to leave them. Next morning the roadman found the dead fox at the mouth of the conduit, and Scurry lying curled up beside him growling savagely. Poor Scurry was badly bitten about the throat, and died from loss of blood a week later; the only terrier I have lost so; though, as I told you, Pompey and Tuppence died together of suffocation. I've had them mauled rather badly at times by badgers, which punish terribly. Jock has frequently drawn a badger after bolting or drawing the hunted fox from the same earth. Scamp once bolted the fox from the Cleithaugh 'cundy' into the jaws of the pack, then dived in again and *bolted* a badger."

"Good little Scamp; he knows we are talking of his exploits."

"Of course he does, and he loves to hear us. He's the most intelligent, next to Jock. Jock is getting old now, and only comes out on 'near-hand' days, and often takes half a day only. Tom the feeder told me that last month, at Wolfelee, he had a fast run that blew and distressed him greatly, followed by a subterranean battle of ten minutes. When hounds were moving off for the afternoon draw, Jock repaired to the hilltop, sat down and watched the direction in which they were going, and seeing them pointing away from home, he turned tail and trotted away off to kennel. Intelligent! Why, they are wiser than most men. Jock knows every earth, drain, and hole in the country-side, and the shortest way to them, and often in a chase guesses where it is to lead to and is waiting there to receive us. It is a fact that on one occasion the hunted fox went into a drain just in front of hounds and was immediately ejected by Jock, who had got there before him; and more than once, on our arrival at an earth, we have heard the muffled yap-yapping coming from it that told us he was at work. He does not seem to feel punishment, and the more he is mauled the prouder he seems when taken notice of. Scamp has a custom of going home with hounds after hunting unless he has been punished. If this is so, he comes down to the house of his own accord to have his face bathed and sponged. This is done by one of the maids who is very fond of him, and Scamp remains for one, two, or three days till his wounds are healed, then returns to the kennels. He has been known to do a cute thing more than once. If he wishes to find me or a particular member of the family, or a special horse, he soon gets tired of running

A TERRIER TALK

from one to the other, sniffing at each, so he watches his opportunity till the field is filing through a hunting gate or a narrow lane, when he stations himself at the head and looks at and smells each one as he passes."

"Now, old man, if we sit up later and have any more of this terrier talk, I'll be hearing from you that you have been holding conversation with the little beggars. Come away and roost."

"But I *have* had frequent talks with them!"

CHAPTER IX

BY INVITATION

"Yon sound's neither sheep-bell nor bark;
They're running! they're running! go hark!"
—KINGSLEY.

THE pernicious practice of exchanging letters with each other at the breakfast table, or of reading aloud extracts therefrom, was not usually followed in the family; but on this morning, in the fall of the year, I handed a note to Joanna with some elation, and its contents were instantly proclaimed in a tone of triumph from behind the tea-urn.

"The Duke has granted us a day in his country. His Grace says"—pause for effect—"or rather the note from the Field-master says: 'If you are short of country and would care to have a day in the Crossford side of ours, you might arrange to go early next month, meeting, say, at Marchfield. You can let me know at once, and write to Jimmy Fairbairn so that he may have the earths stopped.'"

The news produced various comments.

"Hooroosh!" came from one end of the table.

"What luck! Very civil of them; must keep my best fresh for that day," from the other; and the boy Bobby, through a mouthful of scrambled eggs, spluttered, "Hope you'll find a fox. Hope there'll be a scent."

BY INVITATION

Meanwhile I was mentally running over the phraseology of my letter of gratitude accepting the good offer, and considering which horses and hounds I would take, with a determination to present the best available appearance.

The announcement duly appeared:—

THE FOREST FOX-HOUNDS WILL MEET AT 10.30 A.M.
ON SATURDAY, DEC. 6, MARCHFIELD
(By Invitation)

All the followers of our little pack looked forward with intense eagerness to the day.

Fortune did not favour the Hunt during the intervening time, for in the last days of November a run of calamities had occurred in rapid succession. Tom Telfer was down with influenza, which scourge had also prostrated the Second Whip and another stable lad; two of the horses were off, and three couple of good working hounds were unfit from various causes.

The eventful morning dawned, and an inauspicious start was made, most unlike what I had pictured and hoped for. Instead of two natty well-turned-out whips and a full pack, old Batters, in rat-catching attire, and a callow stable boy, mustered a diminished pack of twelve and a half couples round a dejected huntsman; old "Royal" was going short, and the "Omega" mare was coughing. Hounds seemed to be sharing the despondency, and things looked far from rosy. But Batters said, "Yin canna ken what's afore yin; oo micht happen on a richt guid day," and the sequel will show that the oracular utterance had in it the spirit of prophecy.

I had been taking my own way with Batters on several points lately, so gave in to him when, on nearing the place of meeting, he suggested a well-known bridle-path as a short cut, saving a mile. It was only across some four or five large open fields, then down alongside a small clump of plantation; so as we were ten minutes behind time, we followed it. A hare got up under our noses and lobbed slowly along into the above-mentioned clump, and though the two terriers cocked their ears and made a dart out, hounds never looked at her, and were as steady as the proverbial rock, and I dreamt no evil. There was a hunting gate close to the corner of the plantation, and the catch-chain was low, necessitating bending well over to reach down to it. I was fumbling with it when, my back being turned to the pack, first the terriers, then one or two young hounds leapt over the wall, and mistaking old Batters' hoarse rate for a cheer of encouragement, one or two more, till, in a surprisingly short time, all had disappeared and were running in chase with a cry that was full enough to have come from the throats of twenty-five couples, and strong enough to bring down the trees about their heads. Galloping down the side of the wall to the low corner, I was just in time to see a scared-looking fox jump on the top of the wall, and with a twist of his brush, as quickly jump back again. He must have done this almost into the jaws of his pursuers, and from the redoubled chorus I judged they had got a view of him. One turn round and he broke

With a twist of his quarters flung himself over with a foot and a half to spare.

at the bottom with eight and a half couple close at him; and the complexity of the situation was apparent when I realised that the smaller portion of the pack left behind were also in chase, and running backward in the opposite direction. Shouting to old Batters to go on with these and stop them, hearing his fervent "Heeven help us, this is a queer beginnin'," and catching a glimpse of the "Omega" mare dancing on her hind-legs, her petrified rider clasping her round the neck, I went off in pursuit. The first fence was a high unswitched hedge with a low rail in the corner under a tree—a place for any hunter to pop over leisurely and temperately. Not so my old "chaser." He went at it full tilt, and with a twist of his quarters flung himself over with about a foot and a half to spare, crashing my head into the branches, scratching my face, and hooking my scarf round under my ear. Two more fences, and then a big 120 acre park, across the middle of which the little pack sped, revelling in a scent that enabled them to carry a high head, and race along screaming with joy, to my consternation apparently making straight for the front door of the mansion-house. A little mob of Highland bullocks, with wild looks, joined in the chase, carrying their tails erect and galloping like thoroughbreds, and momentarily checking hounds; and whoops and yells from the assembled field testified that the fox was in view.

Close under the stackyard and hinds' houses hounds ran, a dogcart wheeling on the road and some grooms with led horses being swept into the chase, while the laird of Marchfield was heard shouting lustily, "My horse! my horse! or any horse; let's have some sort of horse!" and was soon thundering along.

What a plight for an anxious recently fledged Master of Hounds to find himself in. Instead of the dignified and conventional entry so often rehearsed, to appear on the scene in this headlong fashion. Yet I could not help enjoying the humour of the thing, though I saw with some dismay that we were following hounds that appeared to be tied to their fox, running in a direction away from the country where we were expected, and where some important members of the field would be waiting; and I also thought with apprehension of Batters and the boy away with one-third of the already too small pack making for the hills.

The laird came up, cutting a comic figure, hatless, breathless, with stirrups six holes too short, and crouching like an American jockey in his saddle, and shining with excitement.

"They're running down by the river side and are like crossing, and they're going to kill him," he gasped.

But when we jumped the next fence and got down to the banks we found the panting pack marking at the mouth of a stone conduit. Asking the laird where the other opening was, he said, "It leads into a tile pipe which, I believe, comes away from my laundry. Anyhow, I lost a ferret here lately, and it was found there after the terrified laundry-maid had run screaming to the gardener that there was a serpent poking its nose out of a grating behind the tubs."

"Then, of course, we'll have to leave him and

get back and see where the rest of the hounds have run to."

"You've got another fox on foot, and a chase going on, have you? Well, you are a greedy chap; won't one at a time satisfy you? How, when, and where did you find this one?"

It was only civil to go through the form of apologising for an appearance so sudden and precipitate, and for the dishevelled state of the huntsman; but this was not listened to.

"I wouldn't have missed it for the world," said the laird; "I never had such a piece of fun; you certainly let us know you were coming, and when I heard you I ran to get a horse. I would have been at their tails, but the first horse I got at had a lady's saddle, and the next I seized was this—a fine fencer and a bold one, but I don't know whose he is—how do you like my seat, eh? But how did you do it?"

"Well, laird," I explained, "if you will plant a brace of foxes right in the path, you can't blame hounds for chasing them."

"Now, Master, don't try to make me believe you were not drawing for him."

And it was useless to contradict.

During our short jog back to the house, we were amused to find various ardent sportsmen aimlessly scouring across the country towards all points of the compass, in much anxiety and uncertainty, which was increased by the fact that wild blasts of the horn were being wafted down wind from a direction contrary to that in which we had so unexpectedly flashed. Old Batters was evidently doing his best.

When ultimately we got cooled down and readjusted, and, having appointed two whips for the day, were proceeding to the pre-arranged draw, we met him coming back with his four couples. I could see him glancing at my saddle as if expecting to find a mask there, and from his triumphant expression I half expected to see one dangling from his. He reported having run over a tremendous big country, and having made a five to six mile point (extended in the saddle-room that night, for the benefit of the convalescing grooms, to ten miles, but in reality proved to be one and a half), and implying the exercise of great cunning and desperate racing—(on old "Safety") he cut in before them and stopped them.

Subsequent proceedings kept us on the go all day till darkness overtook us, for we were fortunate in being blessed with a good scent that lasted, and enabled the hounds to run, if not as fast, at least as unerringly at 3 P.M. as they did at 10.30 A.M.

After trying a considerable extent of country, we got on to a fox who, with a ten minutes' start, took us to the hills and down the adjoining valley for a short distance, and attempting to climb the hill on the return journey, failed, and was pulled down in the open in twenty-five minutes.

The shooting tenant of the ground then piloted us to a thick bracken bed where he had often seen a fox that used to lie close to his puzzled setters, and sure enough he was there to-day, and gave a pretty find as he jumped up in the middle of and twisted through the hounds, one or two actually snapping at him. This fox gave a good deal of trouble, for being blown in the first ten minutes' burst, he did not go straight, but took to running short, and attempted every known ruse to baffle hounds, and if scent had not held well he might have succeeded.

He first tried creeping the tops of the stone walls and lying down on the shingles. He then went back to his kennel and pushed up another fox not a quarter of a mile from where he was found; but hounds did not change, and hunted him down into the low country, where he went into a cover and ran his foil. At last he made a quick and curious turn, and ran the road for three-quarters of a mile, bringing hounds to a check. Altogether they hunted him hard for nearly two hours, being very close at him more than once. His fate was an unusual one. Two collies and a greyhound broke away from their master, watching from a hilltop, and killed him stiff and draggled on a bare hillside, just short of a large whin cover generally holding one or two of his kind, and not three minutes in front of a disappointed and eager pack, and a hot and sulphurous huntsman.

But in reality the incidents of this notable day, satisfactory as the authorised programme was, do not obliterate the recollections of the unexpected fun of the morning which is always uppermost.

Old Batters seemed to think the part he played was of the most supreme importance, and on the long jog home repeated it again and again.

"They ran terrible fast, an' the mere gaed like stoor an' lap like a deer. A wud stoppet them suinner, but oo cam till a stane dyke five feet high or mair, vera near, an' the saucy auld bezzom refused it *the first time*. The callant, puir body, was for pushin' the stane aff the cope, bit A telt him there was nae time for that; then oo crossed the Cessburn road in-an'-oot" (through gates), "an' A watched ma chance an' rammed the auld mere forrit owre a stiff railin' an' raced her in afore them, an' whuppit them aff. Aye, they wad killed him in anither quarter mile if A hadna hindered them."

And the genial laird seldom fails to remind me how I came to Marchfield "by invitation."

CHAPTER X

CUMMANSHEMENSLAIGE

> "*Should not his care
> Improve his growing stock, their kinds might fail;
> Man might once more on roots and acorns feed.*"
> —SOMERVILE.

IT was the jubilee of the Talladale Farmers' Club, and the occasion was being celebrated in a characteristic fashion. There had been a 4 P.M. heavy dinner of broth, joints, and plum pudding, to which I and a friend had been invited. It was a somewhat solemn and silent function, and ominously temperate. Then the tablecloths were swept away, and rummers and glasses, with basins of lump sugar, were placed on the table, and bottles of whisky in profusion, apparently in the ratio of one bottle to three men, were set down, while large black kettles of boiling water were handed round by waiting-maids before being placed by the fire.

The loyal toasts were given and received with great heartiness; after which pipes were stuffed and kindled, and a loud hammering and applauding accompanied the rising of the Chairman to propose the toast of the evening—"Prosperity to the Farmers' Club." He spoke with a voice clear as a cornet, and began by addressing his expectant hearers as "Brother farmers all, high and low, that is, hill men and low country men; few if any of you have seen the span of years, or experienced the variety of seasons, or weathered the severity of storms, that I have during the period of my occupancy of the farm of Buccleuch; and few can make the boast which I can, viz. that for two long leases, or rather for thirty-nine years, I have never missed paying my rent punctually and in person.

"I can only touch on some few of the changed conditions during that period. First of all, the system and practice of husbandry is kept up to a high standard, and the most is got out of the land that it will yield; but this only with the expenditure of much capital, with the exercise of much skill, and through the results of oft-repeated experience. But there has been a marked decrease in value of produce of all kinds, the returns from all classes of farms showing a decided falling off from the average of preceding years. This decrease has been in greater contrast in the case of secondary and inferior produce (good articles, whether grain or live stock, never feel the fall so much as inferior articles), and this would seem to point to the importance of keeping our land in good heart so as to grow the best possible crops, and to breed and feed only the best possible animals.

"Accompanying the fall in prices, we have had to pay more for our working expenses, and for nothing so much as labour. The introduction of machines has done away with some of the extra labour formerly employed for harvesting and at odd times, and that has to some extent caused people to move into the towns; but one of the real and main causes of rural depopulation lies in the restless spirit of the age, and the desire of the people themselves. I would counsel the ploughman to pause before he gives up a house rent free, which is kept up for him, his cow, his pig, his hens, and his money wage, paid regularly rain or shine, and moves into the town, where, though wages for himself and his family may be better, the expense of living is out of all proportion higher.

"A new feature of rural life is the invasion of even the remotest districts by so-called grocers' vans. These are very detrimental to farming life, bringing as they do tinned meats, patent medicines, and cheap literature; none of which are so wholesome as the oatmeal and milk or the old books and papers. One class does not change a great deal, and that is the shepherds, more notably the hill shepherds. A good man who can mow, cast peats, and cut sheep drains is always sought for.

"If, then, we breed good stock we shall yet for a while hold our own; and if we are left freedom of contract, and if the transfer of land is made easy and cheap, even under the many adverse conditions we suffer from, we shall be able to keep up the good repute of Border farming, and maintain the high standard of Border live stock."

He gave some most interesting reminiscences of his youth, and of the habits and customs of the hill farmers, and told some very droll stories of sayings and doings at the annual kirns, and wound up by again charging us to be pointed in stock-breeding, and punctual in payment of rent.

Toast and song followed in quick succession. Pat Murray, a jovial-looking young fellow, sang a pathetic song in a way that nearly made us all weep; and his pal, John Fraser, a sad-looking soul, sang one of the most comic of comic songs with the drollest pantomimic gestures.

Then the Croupier rose to propose a toast, and my neighbour whispered that this person had three or four long words which he dragged into every speech he made, and offered to lay me five to four that he would use them all to-night. "Ventilate" and "obfuscate" had at one time been prime favourites, but had long been discarded as being no longer impressive; and the others, which I was soon to hear, were of a similar nature. He was a preternaturally solemn-looking old gentleman, wise as he looked, and very outspoken; and it was with some trepidation that I gathered he was proposing the toast of Fox-hunting, and addressing his remarks to me, as if challenging contradiction. He was sure the present Master was not one to desire to connect, still less amalgamate, the sport of fox-hunting with that of horse-racing and its concomitant gambling, for the two were diametrically dissimilar and ran counter the one to the other; the first being a wholesome and natural recreation, and the last being an unhealthy and artificial method of producing excitement. He wished to promulgate his opinion far and wide that he loved the one and abominated the other—in fact, he looked upon the gambling element of the latter as the "incarceration" of the devil. (Loud applause.) He wound up by hoping his hearers would homologate his sentiments and drink to "Fox-hunting." He apparently added something more, but his closing remarks were drowned in a wave of applause that swept round the table, gathering increased force as it reached my neighbourhood, and carrying several glasses off the table.

Two excited lads sprang to their feet, then upon their chairs, and lastly in emulation upon the table, to second the Croupier's toast. The more likely-looking competitor was hauled down, along with several bottles and decanters; and the other, a rather shy, awkward-looking youth, was held in position and charged to " spit it out." A half tumbler of raw whisky was handed up to him, and this he swallowed at a gulp without winking, and then declared the one thing that induced him to offer for his farm, lying in the forsaken and remote locality it did, was the fact that a pack of fox-hounds hunted within reach. He worked hard all summer, staying at home, while he sent his wife to Spittal-on-Tweed. Here his intimates jeered derisively, for the lady in question was known to do exactly as she pleased. He took his holidays in winter, on the Saturdays with the hounds; and this relieved the monotony, enlivened the existence, and brightened the dark days between Martinmas and Whitsunday. He met his friends, compared notes with them as to the condition of their stock, the stage of their farm work, and sometimes galloped over their young grass and knocked down their fences in return for similar compliments paid to him. He was always pleased to see hounds and a good field, for whom he always had a fox in his whin cover, and a cut of mutton ham and some mountain dew to wash it down. He was applauded to the roof.

My reply was much interrupted by " Hear, hears " —the audience was in a mood to cheer, and cheer they did; so that if there was a fox within three miles of the Cross Keys that night, he must have shivered in his kennel.

The company then broke into knots of three and four, and conversation was very animated, being carried on by some in confidential whispers, and by others in loud declamation that might have been mistaken for quarrelling, but was only meant to emphasise the various propositions laid down.

The fun was at its height when I noted a hard-featured hill farmer, whom I only knew by sight, trying to fix me with his eye. When he had caught mine, he pushed a gigantic tortoise-shell snuff-mull into my hand. After accepting this form of hospitality, and returning the mull, I found him alongside of me, and was puzzled by his repeating again and again—" Will ye cummanshemenslaige, cummanshemenslaige?"

A mutual friend translated the mystic utterance, which turned out to be " Come and see my ensilage," an invitation to inspect the contents of a silo which he had recently established to his own satisfaction and his neighbours' wonder and contempt. He was very old-fashioned and conservative in most respects; but occasionally made an outbreak into modern experiments, and this was his latest departure.

Promising to " cummanshemenslaige " on Saturday, and being adjured to be in good time in a manner so earnest as to draw up a picture of the possibility of the silo going off in spontaneous combustion before then, and being reminded that " Saturday was to-morrow, and that to-morrow was Saturday," we made our escape about 1 A.M.

Friday was spent in kennels, which were visited by several belated sportsmen, one or two of whom let out the fact that the jubilee celebrations were still in progress.

The puddles were covered with a thin coating of ice as we left the courtyard on Saturday morning, and they crackled sharply under "Merrylass'" feet as she stepped briskly away; and where the sun had touched the road, the mud flew in thick flakes from the wheels of the dog-cart; and all human and horse foot-marks were clear and distinct on the slight peppering of snow that had dusted the country overnight. My companion was a young Australian, just home from the back blocks of Queensland, and much interested in all the signs and symptoms of rural life, and an experienced tracker.

After leaving the village we came suddenly upon the youth, John Fraser, one of the most hilarious of the revellers of two nights ago. He was leading a cob without a strap of harness on him by the simple expedient of a muffler round its neck, and was carrying a driving whip. He explained that the cob's forelock had come away in his hand, and he exhibited the tuft in confirmation, but offered no explanation why he happened to be leading it by so frail a medium. He evaded answering all questions as to how he came to be reduced to this pass, merely stating that he was returning to the town. He was grateful to the Australian for showing him a way of leading an unwilling horse by a noose of whip-cord passed round the lip and lower jaw under the tongue, and known to bushmen as the "humane twitch." He inquired, rather anxiously, what road we were taking, and refused all offers of assistance.

About a mile further out, on rounding a corner, we saw John's boon companion, Pat Murray, sitting complacently on a dog-cart cushion, alongside his trap, with the harness piled on the ground, and a horse-rug wrapped round his knees, smoking his pipe. Pat was as communicative as his pal had been reticent, and cried out, in answer to our query what was wrong, that he and John had cast out badly over the questionable soundness of a cob that John had almost sold to him; that they had agreed that a continued journey in each other's company would be deteriorating to both; that this being decided, John had taken out his cob and proceeded to lead him off, when Pat reminded him that the harness was his, and he would rather it was left with the cart. John had demurred to this, but Pat had insisted, so there was nothing for it but to comply, and march off with as much dignity as could be put into the action of dragging a snorting unwilling beast along by the nose and the forelock. John had returned to claim his whip, giving an opening for a reconciliation, but Pat had been obdurate, and had laughed loud when "the Mugger," drawing back from the whip, had left his forelock in John's hand and trotted off, nose and tail in the air; nor did he assist in the capture of the animal, but shouted out, "We'll see who'll be home first." He, too, declined all offers of help, saying he was all right and would soon be picked up by a passing chance.

So we continued our journey, and the Australian exclaimed: "I have been studying the tracks on the road, and there has been some loose driving here, and not so long ago, for they are quite fresh;" and as we proceeded he said, "Will you go slowly here, and let me examine them?"

Our road now branched off to the left from the main valley, and lay across an unfenced moor, and the powdering of snow showed every mark conspicuously, which my friend read like a book.

"Look here," he said, "this chap has been galloping hard and swaying from one side of the road to the other," as he pointed out tracks now running close to the shallow ditch close to the bank, and now perilously near the edge, where a row of stones was all the parapet to guard a wheel from going over the ten foot drop into a watercourse on the other side. "It's a broad flat-tyred trap, probably a grocer's van, and there is another lighter trap, with narrow round tyres. And, by Jove, the fellow has been racing—at any rate the rear trap has been flogging and trying to pass."

Sure enough, a whip broken through the whalebone, and marked as if it had been run over, lay across the road, and Moncrieff's surmise appeared to be correct, for the tracks now showed a less rapid pace and straighter going. At the foot of a hill the sharp eyes of the tracker picked up a cap by the side of the road, and shortly after this the two traps seemed to have pulled up, for the road was paddled with footmarks, and strewn with countless spent matches.

At the end of the road leading through the ford

to the snug farmhouse of Nether, or Under, Fawhope, stood Jim Peebles waiting for us. We had barely pulled up when, anticipating the question, he at once said: "We only got home from the dinner this morning just before daylight, and what a job I had with my cousin, William Peebles. We left the Cross Keys at closing time last night, but we put in at the Doctor's for an hour or two, leaving there about three or four o'clock. William maintained that his pony could out-trot my mare, giving me half a mile start, and I set off before him, and about the crossroads he came galloping and barging behind me like at a bumping boat race, and I had to gallop to save my dog-cart from being crashed into. He was for coming in here, and his pony would hardly pass the road end, and set my mare on jibbing at the ford, and when I hit her she flung up to the dash-board, a thing I never knew her do before. But come away, Upper Fawhope is only three-quarters of a mile on, and we'll just be in time for lunch."

He strode after us with the long swinging stride of a hill shepherd, and kept up to "Merrylass'" quick walk without effort. We found William Peebles sitting on a stone at the turn off of his road, watching a young lad who was applying a liberal wash of whitening to a row of large stones marking the turn.

"Good morning, gentlemen," said he. "These stones are not easy seen on a black night. The last time Jim Peebles was in here he drove over most of them; I see his tracks." And he added half hesitatingly, "They might be useful to you going out to-night."

"Here is your whip, William," said his cousin, coming up. "Mr. Moncrieff found it below the cross roads."

"I must have dropped it when I got out to look for my cap."

We remembered there had been an interval of about a mile between the whip and the cap, but we said nothing.

"I couldn't find the second step of my trap," he continued, "and slipped and cut my head a bit."

"Mr. Moncrieff here says there is a very wobbly driver in the valley, William—a man who drives a flat-tyred broad wheel."

"Ah, ah, Jim, that's you; ye mind ye had your wheels new ringed by Robbie Tamson just a fortnight since. Mine has a narrow round tyre, and makes a track like a velocipede. But open the gig-house and we'll see it."

The gig-house doors were opened, and there stood Jim Peebles' cart, and in the stable an unconcerned-looking boy was wiping down Jim Peebles' mare. William gasped and looked as if he might have explained away the cart, but the two together, cart and mare, were too weighty evidence against him; so producing his snuff-box, removing his cap, and displaying a bandaged head, he said, "Well, that accounts for the bezzom reisting on the hill and cutting across the grass at the corner. But," he added, with confidence, "I'll take my davy that I started in my own trap. We must have changed them when I was looking for my whip, for I mind kindling a match there and sheltering it from the wind with my cap."

We lunched lavishly; and two more hill farmers having stepped in, we listened attentively to the characteristics of hoggs and gimmers and t'winters and dinmonts till it was discovered to be too dark to inspect the silo; but Jim, the lad, was instructed to put a cut in the dog-cart for us to carry home. This we did as far as the first ravine, into which Moncrieff tossed it with his ungloved hands, declaring he would never be able to taste Gorgonzola cheese for the rest of his life.

CHAPTER XI

A HOUND HAVER

"*He guides them in covert, he leads them in chase,*
Tho' the young and the jealous try hard for his place,
'Tis 'Bachelor' always is first in the race;
He beats them for nose and he beats them for pace;
Hark forward to 'Bachelor.'"
—WHYTE-MELVILLE.

THE frost was holding and getting keener, and it was difficult to get horses exercised, for there was not much snow; so hounds were physicked and their coats dusted with sulphur; and we took to curling. Billy did not care much for the game, but rode out to the pond and came home with me. Our horses had frost nails in their shoes, and we were able to jog slowly along the crackling roads, making as much noise as would an artillery waggon. As we approached the out-buildings behind the stable we heard a scrimmage of some sort going on, and Billy said, "My word, those tom-cats are having a battle royal!"

"Chut, Bill, it's two foxes fighting."

And sure enough, as we came round the corner we saw two long forms separate and pop over into the deep glen behind the kennels.

There was more frost and snow during the night, and the morning was spent in the kennels. To Tom the feeder we related the incident of the night before, and that worthy's reply was, "Oh! that's nothing, sir. The foxes were barking and fighting at the gallows over the bones so loud two nights ago that they wouldn't let the hounds get to sleep, and I had to get up twice with the lantern to them!"

We gazed at the huddled-up forms on the sleeping benches, and they were heaped closer than usual during this cold weather. I tested Bill's knowledge by asking him to tell which hound the smallest portion of exposed surface belonged to, and this we did by spelling; for if we had named them, it would have made the hound named uncurl himself and disturb at least two or three of his fellows; so it was—

"What's that lying with his head on R-a-m-b-l-e-r-'s flank?"

"That's P-i-l-g-r-i-m—no? Then it's P-i-r-a-t-e."

"That's right. Now find D-e-x-t-e-r, and so on."

Tom told how some hounds "bossed the benches" and always had their own favourite to make a pillow or a footstool of; how some were liked and some disliked by all the others; how much space was needed before feeding, and how much more after feeding; and many other items of supreme importance in his own eyes.

"I like to see them best when they are tired and fed after a long day's hunting; how they do snuggle up and snore; and when I look in last thing at them not one of them looks up but Regent, and he only opens one eye. Except on the night after a hunt, he's the restlessest beggar ever was, and as he will lie at the back of the bed, and must get up at the least outside noise, he often disturbs the lot. And

We gazed at the huddled-up forms on the sleeping benches.

then they disturb me," he added half shamefacedly.

"I daresay you dream of hounds," said Billy to Tom, as the latter was going off to dinner.

"Well, very often, sir. The other night I dreamt they were all hunting me, and I couldn't run a yard and broke into a cold sweat as Forager drew close up to me."

When the kennel-man had gone I had a score of questions to answer.

"Which is the best all-round hound?"

"Well, Bill, I don't think there's any best of all; there's three or four couple best of all, and each good in a different way. There's Woodman, who will draw find, challenge; then hunt, speak, and drive; and is patient and untiring at a check: not so brilliant, perhaps, as Regent, but more reliable. Regent of course is grand for dash and drive and tongue; but sometimes he is too free, and again is sometimes too fast and gets away by himself. We have more than once come upon him, having run up to the fox, sitting and keeping him at bay till the others came up; for, curiously enough, the poor chap has no teeth at all, and though he is plucky enough, he cannot tackle the fox to any purpose. He is very quick at a check, and always makes a bold wide forward cast down wind first, and then a similar up wind one, and he is nearly always the first to recover it. Of course, he is the best-known hound in the pack, being so prominent and 'kenspeckle' with his rough coat and his white colour, a colour that is most useful, as you can often pick him up against the dark heather at a distance when the others are invisible. Some of the shepherds have said to me: 'A see ye ha' gotten a "beardie" amang them; he'll be mair gleg as the feck o' them.' I wish I had a few more like him."

"Pirate, is that?"

"Yes; alongside of Dexter. Those two are at their best in a straight-out chase; don't try very well sometimes, and are too eager for a start—that is, they don't work a fox close in a big thick cover to push him out; but they, along with Challenger, are always first out; demons to drive a straight-going fox; run consistently at head and keep there until the finish. They are not the least jealous of each other—in fact, seem to work to each other; but I fancy I have seen them a little jealous of the rest."

"A little light of tongue, Challenger, isn't he?"

"He has plenty, but it's soft and very high-pitched, and although he's always using it, on a windy day you don't always hear him at a distance; but as he is generally with those other two and Regent, who all speak freely, it's not felt as a fault."

"A bad point in a pack is a mute hound, eh?"

"The worst sort of all, and not to be tolerated for a day, however good he may be in all other respects."

"But you can't complain of this now, for the last time they ran down the glen, and only twelve and a half couple out, every hound was speaking freely. It positively made me tingle all over, and the cry might have been from twenty couple of throats."

"Yes; they're all right for tongue."

"Sometimes a little slack in drawing, eh?"

"Well, if they are, I put that down to the fact that the country is so well stocked with foxes (in the early season, anyhow); every bit of cover seems to hold him, and they have no trouble to find him. It's mostly a case of 'Hooi in there!' and the fox goes off at the farther end, so that the careful drawers and triers don't get a good start. Ruffian and Royal, for instance, on some days, if they think there is a fox in a strip of plantation say, I've seen them put their noses up and race through it in a straight line."

"Do you like to get away with a few hounds close behind a fox?"

"Yes; I generally go. Though I don't like it, least of all from a close thick whin, because the honest hard-working hounds that have shoved into the thickest parts are at a disadvantage in the matter of a start, and the skirting hounds get away on better terms. But I don't believe in waiting for hounds to come out. If you wait for them, they expect to be waited for, and become apt to dwell; whereas once left behind out of the fun and having to gallop hard to catch up, they take jolly good care not to hang back and be left behind again."

"But don't it disgust them and make them lose interest in trying to find?"

"No; I don't believe it. They are all mad keen to find him and run in chase, and the sooner it comes to that the better. Then, in this country, foxes find themselves so often, and often lie out and rise from the plough or the rough ground."

"I suppose some are better finders than others?"

"Yes. There's gallant little Woodman, my favourite if I have one, he has the knack and has found more foxes by himself than any other. He seems to know where they are lying and goes straight to the spot.

He is most careful, and tries every yard of the ground. I'm sure he has never missed one. He was once or twice left with a bad start; but now he's away like a dart with the best of them."

"I see you let them alone at a check?"

"Yes; most decidedly, unless they have tried wide all round and are completely at fault, and then only do I help them if I have positively correct knowledge of his line; for if they are helped too often they will expect to be helped. Besides that, in this country you can't always get to them on account of wire, or those deep glens, and you must leave them alone; and in my humble opinion this is what makes these hounds work so hard at a check and hunt so close and determinedly. Each wants to be first to recover the lost line, and acts independently on that account. All I like to do is to turn my horse's head in the direction I wish them to try, and move quietly along. It's no use having them shouted at or rated when they are all doing their level best."

"Then, what about a mixed pack?"

"Well, we've always hunted a mixed pack; twelve couple at least of dog hounds and five or six of bitches seems to be a useful proportion. Of course, in an open and flying country I'd like an all-bitch pack; but here the first essential is tongue—without it you'd be looking for hounds all day; for dog hounds are freer and stronger in this respect. They may not be so quick and handy as their sisters, and you may get a stubborn or 'dour' one occasionally, but on a cold scenting day, with a twisting, short-running fox, I think they are more reliable; for their sisters on a cold line might be apt to flash and be more impatient.

But a few couple hunting and running with them sharpens up the dog hounds, I think, and perhaps the spirit of emulation is roused more by their presence. Of course, one has to keep a few more to take the place of those that are laid up in spring, and in the closing weeks we often have an all-dog pack of fourteen couple."

"I see my little friend, Rosebud; she is surely out of condition?"

"Well, you see, she was left behind at the hill farm to have her whelps; then she was brought back to kennels on a cart in a large crate, with her five puppies six weeks old. They were soon afterwards weaned, and a week or so later Rosebud was taken out for exercise with the hunting pack, and shut up at the place of meet to be let out in the afternoon to find her way back to kennel. On getting home later I found a wire from Peter Amos saying Rosebud had come on there—to the hill farm—about six o'clock P.M.—a distance of nineteen and a half miles on the map from where she had been let out."

"Poor old lady," said Bill; "I suppose she was looking for her whelps, and expected to find them there. S'pose she's good in her work like her mother, eh?"

"Yes; but not quite so good. She inherits most of Rosamund's good qualities, and she and her brother Rambler both inherit many of their mother's little tricks and habits. They both on the roads like to be a sort of vanguard about twenty-five yards in advance and on the off-side, and to jump into every water-trough they come to, as Rosamund did. As they are rather handsome, and have a

H

fine carriage, and are as alike as two peas, I don't insist on their being kept in the cluster. Then Rambler invariably carries the mask or nose home; and if he can't get that, a pad; just as his mother used to do."

"Funny how hounds sometimes miss seeing the hunted fox when they have run up to him and he has lain down?"

"Well, I think they are so intent on their noses, as it were, that the other senses suffer to some extent. You've seen, I daresay, hound after hound so bent upon carrying on the line as to run full tilt into wire netting which they would have jumped or avoided had they not been so engrossed; and you've seen them run a line up through a wood while the fox ran back parallel to them quite openly and within a very short distance; and I've seen the whole pack actually run right over the top of a crouching fox without being aware of it. I sometimes think that once the olfactory power is excited and stimulated to full operation the scent penetrates through the eye, through what anatomists would call the lachrymal duct, to the smelling nerve, as well as through the nostrils. Anyhow, it is believed by naturalists that some deer possess this faculty. If you hold any object to them they feel it not only with their noses but with the corner of their eyes where the lachrymal duct opens. Anyhow, hounds don't see so well when they are carrying a head and in full chase on a hot holding scent, as they do when their smell nerves are not stimulated and excited. And it is as well they don't get taken off the line, for the whole essence of hunting is to get hounds to find a line, carry it, and never leave it."

Said Bill: "I once saw a curious instance of this intentness with the Duke's. Hounds had brought their fox very blown into a small whin cover where they were pressing him hard and he was crawling along the top of a low bank alongside a patch of thin whins, when a big powerful hound coming to the cry met him and grabbed him and proceeded to shake and worry him. While this operation was going on the whole pack swept past, paying no attention to it, but racing along on the line which the fox had travelled about three minutes previously.

Pause for a few minutes. Then a question—

"What is the principal cause of the hounds missing a fox after having run him hard and being close at him?"

"Well, I suppose it's more often a failing scent or owing to the fox lying down and keeping perfectly still; so long as he doesn't move he is quite safe, unless a hound happens to blunder against him and shift him. But a very frequent cause with us is the changing to a fresh fox. This would not happen so often if onlookers or others would keep quiet, but so often a run fox is seen to enter a cover and *a* fox is seen to leave it. This last is at once taken for the hunted one and holloaed away by some one who ought to know better. My experience is that the sore-pressed and hunted fox gets to a stage when he does not show himself; his only hope of escape is to hide, which he can do, and does do, in the most unexpected place, and in the most complete manner. It's the fresh fox that shows himself in most cases of this sort. He has digested his night's supper and had a sleep, and now feels fresh enough and bold enough to risk a game of romps, and goes off with no attempt to conceal himself."

"Is there any way of telling from the hounds if they have changed?"

"Well, I sometimes think that if, say, three or four couple have been running steadily at head during a chase, backing each other and without jealousy and with a regular cry, and when they run through a holding place, and all at once these hounds stop speaking and a fresh lot join in with a noisy cry, this may be sign of a changing scent with a change of fox."

A shrill whistle from outside the yard and a voice piped up—

"Whatever have you been doing? It's 2.30, and lunch is cold. Fie, fie—wasting time!"

"Don't say we've been wasting time; we've been having a grand 'hound haver.'"

CHAPTER XII

SOME BY-DAYS

*"See that old hound,
How busily he works, but dares not trust
His doubtful sense, draw yet a wider ring;
Hark now again the chorus fills."*
—SOMERVILE.

MANY of our best gallops and finest hunts have taken place on by-days or days snatched unexpectedly in the middle of a frost, when it had given sufficiently to be safe for horses' legs and hounds' feet, and very often on the day before it settled down again with more than its former severity. And after a carefully kept record of the weather conditions in relation to scent, I can only learn this, that we've had an unfailing good scent just before the oncoming of a hard frost, and generally on a light east wind day with a rising but not too high barometer. Upon the month depends a good deal; and perhaps during February, when the ground is drying not too fast, more straight-out fast gallops occur than in any other; but scent may be good in any month provided the weather is not too unsettled and changeable.

The most notable of days snatched from the arms of the frost was that on which "the grey fox of

Ruberslaw" gave such a fast and straight chase, over an unusual line, if not a very long one.

It was on the 25th January, the beginning of the period when good hunts are expected, and a good scent is assured. Hounds had found in the rocks, and luckily were above the fox when he ran down west of the seedlings by West Lees and crossed the river above the keeper's house, hounds following slowly till they crossed. The Bedrule shepherd viewed and holloaed him there; and after that hounds drove hard every yard of the way. They ran up Fulton Hill to west of Bedrule pond, down the old toll strip, across Swinnie to west of Gilliestongues and crossed Bairnkin strip and Bairnkin road in and out, east of the entry, up the Kersheugh and Ford strip to the Flat, without a waver and with a full cry all the time, down to Scraesburgh Moss, then sharp right-handed past the Ford cottages to Mossburnford Bank, where the cry ceased suddenly. Hounds came pouring down to the Ford and started to drink and bathe, and George Dod, who had joined in, began to whoop from the bank, and I saw him lift the fox over the fence out of the wood. He had found him crouching as if in life—in fact, at first he thought he was still alive—with old Marmion lying facing him and growling savagely. He was the finest specimen of a fox I ever saw; in his prime, probably second or third season—long, lean, and limber, with the pointed muzzle of the Cheviot foxes, grey back and magnificent brush. It almost seemed a shame to tear him; and by the time we were ready for it, he was so stiff that when we propped him up on his legs he stood there, and

SOME BY-DAYS

after brush and mask were removed, hounds took a long time to break him up. Though only five miles from point of finding to point of killing, this was a very fast and hard gallop for horses; only Tom Telfer and I were in it; and the features of it were the pace and line, this last being right across the usual country at right angles to the valleys, right across the Rule, right across the Black Burn, and right across the Jed, never swerving or turning up or down the watercourses.

Another day snatched out of the frost's fingers was Monday, 9th December. We had been stopped on the Saturday. Sunday was soft, a little frost on Sunday night, but all gone by mid-day on Monday, when I sallied up the water blowing the horn as I went. This only produced two followers, Miss Douglas and Frank Turnbull. We found a fox in Birkenside, and hounds drove out at the west end; and when we got to Dolphinston we heard and saw them racing beyond Earlsheugh towards the Belling. For forty minutes they hustled him round by Woodhouse, Belling, and Old Jeddart in two big figures of eight, and then killed him in the garden of the latter place. On my coming up I found two couple of hounds only had got in before the gate was shut, and the rest were clamouring and springing at the high fence. As I came in sight I saw an excited farm youth seize the fox, whip out his knife, and with his left hand whack off the brush, bone and all, and flourishing it above his head he yelled like one demented; then, horrible to relate, the fox at his feet gave a last expiring gasp.

After the worthy farmer had refreshed us, and as we

were riding away, I looked back and saw a tall figure in white night-clothes and cap look from an upper window and draw back behind a curtain. To Miss Douglas I said, "Did you see that? Was it a ghost?"

"Well, it must be old Mrs. Shaw; only she's bedridden and not allowed to move, being at the point of death."

The poor lady's death actually occurred a few days after; and meeting her husband later on, I apologised for the disturbance we had created, and expressed a hope that the unusual commotion and excitement had not hastened the end.

"Oh, it disna signify, sir," was his reply; "she was lying and forbidden to rise; but she wad ha' dee'd onywey!"

On one of these by-days we had the longest and latest ride home I had had up till then. After running hard all day and putting two foxes to ground in unassailable strongholds in the Newton-Denholm country, late in the afternoon we moved away towards Cavers to collect the three couples of hounds short. We came on them running a fairly good line outside the big Dene, and of course our pack of eleven couple joined in and went away westwards. This was nearer four than three o'clock, and we could not keep with them owing to the bad riding. There were snow-wreaths at the back of all the fences, with some hard spots, and many of the gates were still blocked. We crossed the Hawick and Newcastle road at High Tofts, and on by Kirkton Hill, Adderstonlee, Adderstonshiels, and Cogsmill, then by Berryfell to Stobs Bank, where we completely lost hounds. My horse was utterly done, reduced to a walk, and Billy and Jack were not much better. They had gone on, and I was wandering slowly up the road by the riverside. My horse was so exhausted that I had to put him into the stable, when a chilled drink and some old bog hay revived him a little. Some boys came to say they thought the fox was "holed" in the bank about a mile higher up the river. I went on and found two young hounds marking in a half-hearted way at the opening of a stone conduit which I knew and feared, because we had never been able to bolt from it. The terrier came up and showed us that there could be no access as, a few yards from the mouth, the roof had fallen in and was blocking it. I kept blowing at intervals, this bringing in two or three couples, all of which were panting and had the appearance of having been recently in chase. By this time it was quite dark, and I was on the point of returning to get my horse, when I heard a faint cry in the distance. This gradually came nearer and nearer, till I realised that hounds were running down the wooded bank of the river and very near their fox. Enjoining the boys to keep perfectly quiet, we held our breath and listened to the approaching chorus. Something glided past on the loose stones above me, followed by the dash of a couple of hounds close behind it; those we were endeavouring to hold broke away and darted after them, then there was a splashing in the river, and a "skirling" as of cats fighting, a hound which had been nipped calling out, then a rush of more hounds almost to my very feet as they flung themselves into the stream and grabbed and tore savagely at the body of the fox that had carried them so far from kennels, and baffled them so completely for a while. It was now 7.15, and, though Jack and Billy turned up very soon, swelling with pride at the part they had played in keeping hounds together, their horses had to be made comfortable before we could start for home. From the keeper's wife we got some real oatcakes or girdle cakes and half a tumblerful of whisky and water before setting out on a fourteen or fifteen mile jog home—twelve and a half miles on the map—and it was fully three hours later before we sighted the stable lantern.

"I see ye've killed him, sir," said Tom.

"How can you tell in this light, Tom?"

"Well, sir, from the way some o' the hounds is swaggerin', an' I think I saw old Rambler carrying the nose as he went past."

Curious finishes to outstanding hunts sometimes take place, and once or twice we were like losing our fox altogether, after having killed him fairly.

On one of the Harwood days we ran a fox out by Wauchope to Cribb's hole, by the Flush to Dykeraw, and in very fast to Tythehouse, where I viewed him one field before hounds, crawling in front of them. When we got up to them at the mill cauld we found hounds were walking round on the tips of their toes, some bloody, some scraping at the apron of the cauld, all with their hackles up and signs of battle, one tuft of fox fur but no fox. Now what to do? Could we put the fox into the count, no one having seen him killed or having handled him? Whipping off some of the boards to let the terrier in disclosed nothing; and only after

Setting out on a fourteen-mile jog home.

half-an-hour's fishing and groping with hay forks and rakes in the deep pool below was the body fished out, and hounds, which had been taken away, were brought back to eat it. Jack the whip's elation was so marked that Billy sought and obtained an explanation of it. He had laid odds that before the end of the month (February) we should have killed fifteen brace, and this made it, though it was only the nineteenth day of the month.

This part of the country was well stocked with stout straight-running foxes, so when it was possible to put in an extra day, I was tempted to do it.

On a day following very closely on the last, a likely-looking beggar, as Tom Telfer described him, found himself in the heather outside Lurgiescleuch, and made for the heights, the hounds soon streaming in a long string after him, and very soon running out of sight. The terrier, and one or two tailed-off hounds, were our guides by Wauchope Common, Hemlaw, Fanna Rig, Note-o'-the-Gate, to Singden, where, in a blown-down plantation of spruce trees, we found hounds hard at work. We obtained the comforting news that the Liddesdale hounds had been through it that morning, so there could only be our fox in it. Very soon after we viewed him steal away on the backward journey, a five and half mile straight point. But this time he kept more to the south, down the bank of the stream, and by Wauchope House they were pressing him closely. On by the Forking and Hawkshaw March they drove with an enlivening chorus, making the whole valley resound, past Hobkirk between the church and the river, then crossing the latter just below the village. Surely he is doomed now! But it was not till an hour later that I took off his brush and threw him to the pack. 'Twas this way. After he had lain down in a ploughed field and hounds overrun him, Pirate and Dexter pushed him up and he made a spurt for the river. Two hounds rushed at him and simultaneously pinned him on the top of a high bank and rolled down into the deep pool, below a sort of fall, where they throttled him and then left him. We could not discover him in the failing light till the pool got smoothed and was free from hounds swimming in it, and until the discoloured water had cleared. Then we got sight of him in about eight or nine feet of water poised on the point of his nose and two fore pads, his brush stretched stiffly out behind him, about six feet below the surface. The pool was enclosed by a shelving bank of gravel which sloped suddenly down into at least twelve feet of depth, and as the fox was, so to speak, suspended exactly in the centre of the pool, he could not be reached from the side with paling bars, and to attempt him from below only meant pushing him into deeper water. My bribe to the assembled boys to strip and dive for him was not responded to, so in the end I waded the "powney" in as far as she would go, and with a crooked wire hooked him; but for some time it looked as if hounds were going to lose the satisfaction of tearing and eating their fox.

Another very satisfactory by-day was a Monday after a very hard Saturday, which had lamed half the pack. I had not the most remote notion of going out—in fact, had fixed on having a day with the Duke's; but from my dressing-room window at 8.15 I saw a brace of foxes walk down a furrow in the plough on the opposite side of the glen and lie down together in a hollow. I saw they could be approached from above by making a big detour; this I did on the pony with only Jack as follower and eight couple of selected sound hounds. It took half-an-hour to get round, and being directed by signal from the bath-room window of the house, I trotted quickly down along the very furrow in which the unsuspecting pair were lying, and the hounds were on the top of them before they knew it. They diverged right and left, the vixen going straight down into the glen, and the dog, to his credit be it said, taking straight across the plough, drawing six couple away from his mate. These six couple hunted him well, sticking closely to him round the Dunion and Bedrule Hill, bringing him back to the glen, where they continued to press him for another half-hour, and being reinforced by all the loose terriers belonging to the establishment, they hunted him from one hiding-place to another until they killed him, about two hours after he had first been viewed. Few of those friends whom I met in the Duke's field about midday, to whom I related my story, seemed to think I was not romancing.

Pleasant as were these by-days, often providing the most unexpected sport and satisfactory finishes, they were seldom so enjoyable as the regular hunting days. Many of the one-horse followers used to go home after a morning's hunt, leaving a few keen spirits to have another try for him. Tom Telfer, Frank Turnbull, Dick Davidson, George Heriot, Tom Smith, poor Archie Rutherfurd, Robert Laing, George Davidson, and others, never left so long as there was light to draw; and being all good horsemen and anxious to go one better than the other, the pace of these afternoon hunts was never slow, and some prodigious deeds of valour were performed.

Not so often did we kill our fox on these occasions, but nearly always hounds ran hard and pressed their fox, very often putting him to ground at too late an hour to admit of bolting or digging.

CHAPTER XIII

A HILL DAY

"*He's away for the moors in the teeth of the wind.*"
—KINGSLEY.

THE interest had not slackened, but the season was waning; hounds were light in condition, some of the four and five season hunters showing signs of loosening of toes and wearing of feet; earths had been opened for some time and drawn out by the vixens who were now lying up dog foxes were getting scarce and not easy to find; lambs (the huntsman's bane) were a full crop and two or three weeks old on the lower farms; scent was uncertain; the country was hard, dry, and dusty; and the weather was of the barren and boisterous character common to the period.

The beginning of the day was unpropitious, for we had lost a quarter of an hour at the start, and none of it had been wiped off by the time we passed the half-way milestone. Old "Safety's" jog was rougher than usual; if there was a loose stone she found it and kept dribbling it in front of her like a footballer till she made her last effort to kick it away, accompanying this with a grunt and a stumble.

The last half of the twelve-mile jog was on a high moorland road, open to the full force of the blast rushing down from the heights; and as we bent our heads to the wind and quickened the pace, I cursed myself for having agreed to give this extra day in this wild waste district on the very outskirts of our country. It had been thought desirable to kill or scare away one or two foxes here before the hill lambing commenced, and though hounds were to hunt the next day on the same side of the country, the fixtures having been duly advertised, this unadvertised by-day had been planned as an auxiliary to it. An amazing number of the keenest of keen sportsmen had assembled at the place of meeting, an exposed farmhouse on a wind-swept hillside, where they were trying to obtain such shelter as was afforded by the walls of a dry-stone sheep-fold. The horses had their tails tucked in and their ears laid back; but their masters' faces, already glowing from exposure, beamed with pleasure at the sight of hounds, and we had a cheery greeting.

The two joint masters of a trencher-fed hill pack rode up from the opposite direction, and I hailed them with satisfaction, for I deemed that their pilotage might be useful before the day was ended. I was relieved to notice they had not brought any of their hounds; but several sharp-looking, hard-coated terriers ran with them.

For nearly three hours we tried all sorts of likely lying places, exhausting all the hitherto known kennels above ground.

"Ye shood ha' been here at seven o'clock in the mornin' an' ye might ha' got a drag," Sandy Oliver kept reiterating. "We'll have to risk disturbing a vixen, and run the terriers through the big earth at Todholes now."

I was loath to do this, but there seemed no other way of getting sport; so blowing the disappointed hounds together, we moved on for the famous earths on the opposite side of the valley.

In passing a patch of heather that had escaped the previous spring's burning, and that was mixed with rough boulders and battered bracken, one or two of the rear hounds hung back, and old Warrior stood still for a moment, feeling the air with his nose before dashing forward, when suddenly, and as if the earth had opened and shot him out, a big supple-looking dog fox projected himself and stretched away like a greyhound, the whole pack screaming after him like distracted beings as he increased his distance from them along the side of the hill.

"That's right, keep out above them," shouted Sandy Oliver, as he cantered past me tying a new cracker on to his thong as he went. "By the Lord, they *are* scolding him along proper. That beats a blooming kirk organ," he added.

For full forty minutes we galloped, or rather scrambled, slithered, or floundered over as rough a piece of country as ever tried the mettle of the stoutest horse. No sooner had we surmounted one hilltop than we saw another before us, higher and farther off than the last, and as we breathed our blowing horses before we set them going again, I heard the shout of one or more of the hill-men, "There they go! Yonder they go! Right forward away!" as they pointed to the expanding sky-line.

I freely confess I was no more anxious to keep in sight of hounds than of the active form of the Master of the Talladale and his pony's rat tail, as he sailed along with little apparent effort. Once I thought I had lost him; but he came skating down a steep face, his pony sitting on its haunches with its forefeet pushed out before it, and shouted, "They're right on, and we'll have to cross the bog. We'll lose them if we go round. Keep close in to the edge of the haggs between the wet and the dry; you'll do fine if your mare knows them." And with that he disappeared between two overhanging haggs into what looked like the bed of a stream.

Old "Safety" had many opportunities of "knowing them" and learning them in the next few minutes, and it was not without several struggles that we emerged on to harder ground.

Three or four more hill-men were now showing in front, and I rode in their tracks, watching them pointing forward with their whips to where you could just see the hounds fading away over the farthest ridge.

Pounding on for another mile or more, I heard loud whoops, and came upon a small knot of excited men, who threw themselves off their horses, leaving them to stand without hobbling or tying up in any way, and rushed down into the hollow where hounds were baying loudly and digging furiously.

"It's only a water-crack," said Dave Oliver, after we had taken hounds off to some distance. "We'll soon bolt him out of there if my brother Sandy's terrier would come up."

"Why not try my whulp?" said Geordie Davidson, producing the said creature from a game bag which he carried.

A HILL DAY

"It's too big and wet, Geordie; he'd never go in."

"Never go in!" yelled Geordie, and a heated argument began, which was only ended by the appearance of Sandy's terrier, who decided the dispute by diving into the crack lower down the hollow, Sandy himself lying prostrate on his stomach on the ground with his ear closely pressed to the earth, while the rest of them drew back and watched with the most intense interest. Sandy's hand went up to indicate he had located the spot from which the yaps and grunts accompanying the subterranean battle proceeded, and he crept softly on all fours down the hollow. Five, ten, fifteen minutes of cold suspense followed, during which a few straggling men and horses arrived, all to take up a position well back and above the centre of attraction. Then Sandy, crawling quietly away, came up to say he could hear nothing, and thought they must be in grips.

"If we had only a spade, we could shift him," he said; "but it's too far to send in to Skaithhill. But what's this? Here come two lads carrying something very like the instrument."

Two wiry shepherds were not long in setting doubts at rest.

"We keep an old draining spade on the heights," they explained; "it often comes in handy."

An opening was soon made, and Sandy's terrier dragged out slightly punished, and at his urgent request Geordie Davidson's young Piper was put in. He wriggled out of sight in a second, and soon after his delighted master was screaming in enjoyment: "Hooi at him, Piper lad, good Piper lad, hooi at him. He's driving him doon the hill is Piper."

"Whist, Geordie; if ye mak as much noise, nae fox will bolt."

A few minutes of expectation, and then I saw Geordie staring as if his eyeballs would burst, and thought I caught sight of a black object slinking down the bed of a small watercourse.

"Ta-a-a-aly-ho!" screamed Geordie, unable to contain himself any longer, and hounds poured away like a cataract.

"Bi ghor, that's a ghrand tarrierh!" said the shepherd; "look yhonderh, he's oot close ahint him!"

What sliding and skating; some going straight down, some at a slant; but all arriving at the bottom somehow.

Old "Safety" sprawled into an innocent-looking green spot; I flung myself off to ease her, and landing half-way up to the knee, left my boot stuck fast in the ground, clean sucked off. The amusement of several of the boys was undisguised, though I did not altogether appreciate the chaff to which I had to submit.

"Using Todshawhope as a boot-jack, Master?" "Suffering from hot feet, sir?" "Boots too tight?" and such-like poor witticisms.

But they were sufficiently Samaritan to catch the old mare, and I pulled the boot out and worked the foot into it, and continued the chase, grudging very much the lost minutes.

I was not above being guided by Sandy Oliver again, who to my surprise turned back towards us with a set expression on his face: "We can't get through the Red Cleugh; we're far better on this side of the hill."

A HILL DAY

"Ta-a-ally-ho! the tarriorh's oot close ahint 'im."

"He'll never make the heights; they're bound to turn in. Come on."

"Lord preserve us," he cried in his excitement, "they must be running in view, and here's that blasted wire fence—the march between Todlaw and Softhope—tightened up and renewed. We'll have to get through it; there's not a gate for miles."

He brought his pony alongside the fence, stepped off and stood on the top wire, balancing himself with his hands on the saddle, dancing and swinging and stamping till a staple flew; then moved along to the next post, and the next one or two, repeating the operation. Then jumping down, he bound the loosened wires tight together with his stirrup leather, and laying his coat on them, he led his pony over, the sensible beast quietly lifting one leg at a time.

"Safety" played the fool, hanging back and planting her toes in the ground, breasting the fence anywhere but the right where, and at last leaping so suddenly and so high in the air as almost to land on the top of me.

Sounder ground enabled us to canter round the base of the hill to a point overlooking the whole of the wide hope below, which we eagerly scanned, but without seeing a sign of the chase.

"They can't be down into Softhope burn below us, or we would hear them, and they haven't had time to get over Red Cleugh heights; they must have put him to ground again," said Sandy.

Emerging from the bed of the stream higher up we now saw Davie Oliver on his white pony, with a few followers, moving in an uncertain way, and apparently as much at a loss as we were ourselves.

But a note on the horn brought several dark forms out of a side cleuch directly below us, and on going down we found the pack at the edge of the stream, most of them lying in it drinking and panting; and a little way off, after some search, a mangled object stretched and flattened and so plastered with black peat as to be more like a fox that had been dead for a week than the limber animal that had just stood up so well in front of hounds.

"They never do break up a fox when they kill him in a peat-hole like that," explained Sandy.

Davie was urged by his elder brother to thrust a finger down the creature's throat, which he did very gingerly, and reported not only that it was blood-hot, but declared he felt an expiring twitch and quiver, with an attempt to close the long jaws, which made him retract his finger with more decision than he had inserted it.

After washing in the stream and removing brush, mask, and all the pads, amid the whoops and yells of their followers, the body was thrown to the hounds, who soon tore him and ate him, being assisted in the operation by such of the terriers as had come up. These determined little creatures held on to and fought for every scrap of skin, and we had a good laugh to see Geordie Davidson's Piper pounce upon a small portion and bear it off while the brothers Oliver's terriers were locked in mortal combat over the same prize.

Estimating distance and time and comparing notes occupied us till we followed down stream to the shepherd's house.

"Where got ye that saddle, Dave?" inquired Sandy.

"It's the Master's. I lent mine to Jack the whip to use to get his horse out of Lairhope bog," said Dave; "he was in firm up to the withers and had done struggling; so, as my saddle was a very old one, I whipped it off, and we turned it up before him and drew the horse's fore-feet out and put them on the panels, and flicked him with our whips, and at the first try he got out. But I bargained that Jack was to ride home on my dirty saddle, and I was to get his."

"And how did you get off Softhope?" pursued Sandy.

"We took down the water-gate, and lifted the hanging rail off," replied Davie; "but you came a quicker road. Where did you get a gate in the march fence?"

"Oh, about half-way down the rig on the other side of the hill," replied his brother, winking at me.

At the parting of the ways we were only one couple of hounds short; but of their followers only nine out of about thirty starters survived, and of these six were hill-bred men on hill-bred horses.

Fourteen miles from our sleeping place, and eight from the point where we were to meet the fresh horses and some four couple of fresh hounds, and it was dusk, and every minute of daylight was precious.

"You'll save nearly a mile and a quarter if you cut across behind Dryslade woods," shouted Sandy Oliver, as he waved back "Good-night."

How I repented of taking this road may be imagined when, five minutes later, hounds, without any warning, dashed off into the sombre woods on a red-hot scent, screaming as if to waken the dead. Blowing till I was blue, my two companions cracking their whips, rating till they were hoarse, and riding their tired horses for all they were worth, produced seven and a half couple of surprised hounds, while the rest pursued with a vigour and a vehemence worthy of a better time and occasion.

"It's no use, Ben; Mr. Stewart and you will have to go back and try to stop them and bring them on to Dryslade farm."

Only those who have tried it can know what an exasperatingly slow process it is to coax tired-out foxhounds with a leg-weary horse along a strange road, especially when their heads are turned away from home, and when you have no one putting them on from behind. Stiff, chilled, and dispirited, I crept along by slow yards, blowing a dejected note on the horn at intervals, musing on the alternating joys and misfortunes of the day, attempting to realise the predicament in which I was placed, and picturing the sort of appearance I would cut next day with only half a pack of hounds.

A faint "Hi, woa!" came from the distance; a figure showed in the dusk running across the fields; then a friendly voice shouted: "Stop, Maister. A've been watchin' ye a' day," it panted, "an' A've seen the feck o' the hunt; ye've hed a lang sair day, an' ye maun bei gey hungery an' awfullies droi, and me an' the wife's socht ye a basket." It was dear old Andrew Waugh, and the basket was a generous supply of scones, and oatcakes, and cheese, and currant loaf, and butter, and a decanter of whisky, and glasses.

"Dod! bit er ye a' yersel? What hae ye dune wi' the rest o' them?" said the honest fellow, as he poured out a generous supply from the decanter. "Michty, what a gran' hunt. A aim gled ye catched him," he went on ejaculating, as his questions were answered by degrees.

Sitting on the bank by a roadside spring of water, when one of the most delicious meals was in progress, the rap rap of horses' feet was heard, and Stewart and the boy jogged up with the missing hounds. Sandy and the rest of the hill-boys had heard the cry approaching them, and by a liberal use of whip-cord and voice had stopped the hounds. So the feast was prolonged, and with the dews falling and the stars coming out we demolished "the basket" and drained the decanter to the toast of "Andrew Waugh and fox-hunting."

CHAPTER XIV

BLANK DAYS, ODD DAYS, AND A RECORD DAY

> " *Who-whoop! they have him, they're round him, how*
> *They worry and tear when he's down!*
> *'Twas a stout hill fox when they found him, now*
> *'Tis a hundred tatters of brown!"*
> —WHYTE-MELVILLE.

IT was an infinite satisfaction, and it had begun to be my boast, that we seldom had a blank day. Often did we draw a good big tract of country in the spring months, when vixens were below ground and dog foxes were lying out in the open, without finding, and often when things were looking hopeless, a fox would discover himself in the most unlikely and unusual spot and provide a good hunt or a fast gallop as the case might be. And even if we had only a short scurry with an "interesting" vixen, whom we speedily put to ground and as speedily left, or if we slowly followed the short turnings of an anxious and crafty old dog fox, till, under cover of night and failing scent, he beat us, there was always some fun to enjoy and some amusing incident on which to look back. Though it was in the first days that the most droll occurrences happened and the most novel situations arose.

One day, an alert-looking little man was seen to dismount and hold open the gate from a turnip-field to allow a somewhat strung out line of riders

to filter through, with the intention of shutting it when the last had passed. A voice from one of the field well in the rearguard was heard to call out to him—
"Go on, go on, don't wait for me."
"I think I'll wait and shut the gate."
"Oh, nevah mind waiting for me."
Still the obdurate person stood at the gate.
"We nevah shut gates when hounds are out," as he approached.
"Well, sir," said the gatekeeper, "as the turnips are mine, and these sheep coming to us are mine, and I believe the —— gate is half mine and half the Yerl o' Whum's, I think I'll wait back and shut it after I get you through, so bustle up, please."

One morning, during a fast gallop over an estate where the fences were well looked after, where jumping places of stout larch rails were put up in what wire there was, and where gaps were few and instantly repaired when they existed, an amusing dialogue took place. We crossed the march or boundary fence, consisting of a fairly high bank with a rail on the top, and as horses were rather blown, most of us were glad to have it at a spot where the fencers were at work renewing the rail, of which they had taken down a rood or two. In the afternoon the homeward way lay back over the same line of country. The foreman fencer, the village joiner, was just about to fix up the last bar, and one of the field seeing this, rode up in advance.

"Hi, Sandy, let's through there before you nail it up."

No reply from Sandy except a roar to a young apprentice to watch what he was doing, and a little more vicious wielding of the hammer.

"Sandy, man, pull that down."

Then Sandy's opportunity came.

"Pull this doon," said he, without removing his pipe; "I'll dae naething o' the kind; we've juist bin sent oot here ti pit it up."

But I once drew blank for Tom Telfer, and of this Joanna was frequently pleased to remind me.

It was in this wise. Tom was staying in the house preparatory to making a very early start by train to hunt next day. I got up in the darkness, and had not proceeded far with my dressing, and was in very scant attire, when I thought I would see if my whip was stirring. So, groping along the passage, at the farther end of which were two doors, I opened the right-hand one, struck a match, and walked across to the dressing-table to light the candles, saying, "Time to get up, Tom." Then suddenly a feminine voice from the pillows said quite calmly and with appalling distinctness, "Hulloa, Master, whatever do you want in my room?" Looking round, I beheld a frizzled-up head, which I only half recognised, and in my agitation shouted, "Where the devil is Tom Telfer?" To which the young lady chillingly replied, "Well, you didn't expect to find him here, did you?" I could only gasp and stare helplessly in the direction of the small crib in the corner of the room, and my dilemma was the worse when the match burned my fingers, and being hastily dropped, left me in black darkness.

There was one part of the country which was getting short of foxes, and which we had drawn blank on two successive days' hunting, and here it was that we had two odd and unexpected hunts on one day.

It was with many misgivings that I proceeded thither in response to the urgent request of the shooting tenant for a third time round. As we passed the door of the keeper's house, that worthy imparted the startling information that "the Talladale dogues had bin rinnin' yammerin' aboot sin grey daylicht." This was the description given of a small trencher-fed pack that occasionally made incursions into our territory on days when we were at the other side, so mischievous persons said.

But there was nothing for it than to go on, which we did at the very moment when a tired and draggled-looking fox crossed the avenue in front of us, of course taking hounds along with him, and with a burst of music that fairly made the tree-tops tremble. They chased him through the rhododendron bushes and once round the garden, and caught him behind the house by the river-side. In the midst of the struggling mass were two couple of strange hounds all peat-stained and travel-soiled, and with long unrounded ears; and after the trophies were saved and the fox was eaten, a heated youth on a panting pony arrived shouting excitedly, "Where's *my* fox?" and was not over-pleased when it was explained to him that *his* fox had been accidentally killed and devoured.

Two futile hours were spent in drawing every bit of holding on this and the adjoining estate all blank, when Tom Telfer's hawk eye caught sight of two horsemen on the sky-line apparently coming in. Holding hounds together, and waiting and watching, we were not long in making out the white form of a light-coloured hound in the distance coming towards us, and making fair progress on the line alone. Our Talladale friends were at work again, and we heard their shouts faintly in the distance as they cheered on the rest of the baying pack. To our undisguised delight we viewed the fox, a rakish-looking hill customer, coming inwards, and we saw him actually pass up wind of us and about a quarter of a mile off. Hounds, if they did not view him also, knew he was there, and were soon screaming in the wake of the astonished animal. He took them at a great pace about three miles straight, and was killed on the steps of the Parish Church Manse. So, for the second time on one and the same day, we ran and killed a fox found by another pack, and on this latter occasion we saved the carcase for the neighbouring Master, who, soon coming up with his lot, had the satisfaction of seeing it eaten by the combined packs.

A RECORD RUN

Far from anticipating a blank day, we felt the full assurance of coming sport, as we started one morning early in the year with the low temperature of 38°, a minimum of 28° during the night, and a light east wind and a rising barometer. For we had received gracious permission to hunt an enviable portion of the Duke's country, well stocked with stout running foxes, and consisting of sound old pastures strongly fenced, and good moorland of unlimited extent, over which we had recollections of many good gallops with his Grace's famous pack.

"I like the feel of things to-day," Billy had said,

A RECORD DAY

sniffing the air as we left the stableyard; and, "I like the look o' things," he added, as we came into sight of about thirty as keen sportsmen as one would wish to join, assembled at the place of meet—a number augmented to about sixty as we moved off to draw Tofts Dene. Hounds had dashed out of kennel that morning and behaved as if they already felt a scent, and now showed indications of wishing to be put into a small strip of plantation on the way to the Dene; and barely waiting for Tom Telfer to slip on to a cross ride or for the wave of my arm, they hurled into it and instantly threw their tongues. I saw Tom's cap go up, and as I got nearer him, noticed the remains of the strangled scream that was half choking him as he galloped forward with set teeth, spurring all he knew and cracking his whip, as he raced for a point where he wished to head the fox off from going back into our own country. This he succeeded in accomplishing, so much to his own satisfaction that his "gone away" holloa was unnecessarily loud and prolonged, and his excitement led him to whip out his horn and blow till his breath was spent.

Tom claimed an intimate acquaintance with every fox in the country-side, and he was wont at times to declare he knew them all by head mark.

"That's the beggar the Duke's chivied on Thursday when they had to be stopped in the darkness at four o'clock, and he's stiff as a board, and stale as cold porridge," he yelled, as I got alongside of him. Then reading disapproval in my eye, he added, "Nothing like giving him a 'gliff' to go away with;

makes him scoot along; nothing like bursting him up at the start."

But Tom was not invariably right in his recognition of foxes, for five minutes later we saw hounds coursing a wretched creature along the river's bank and pull him down in mid-stream as he was trying to cross a shallow, making for a rough scaur in which there were caves large enough to hold a whole pack. When I waded in, half-way up to the tops of my boots, I found a poor beast, unsound on both forelegs—one being snare-marked, and the other carrying a wire that was cutting in to the bone—yet fat as a seal withal, and quite incapable of standing up before hounds, so Tom had to confess himself mistaken.

Before this fox was well broken up we heard a far-off holloa from the top of the Dene, and as we moved off to it, information was conveyed by signal and otherwise that a fox had gone away, and we learned that he had a good six or seven minutes' start.

Hounds, who were keen enough to begin with, were now desperately eager; but we held them together till we got round above the Dene, where they felt for and soon found the line, and went off with a good cry and at a fair pace.

A bunch of so-called "knowing ones," mostly from neighbouring hunts, had ridden cunning for a start, and had the advantage of being above us and on the right side of the stream, and seemed likely to hustle hounds before they had properly established a scent and settled down to run it. But the line was over a nicely fenced country that required a little doing, and one hedge and rail with a ditch to us took toll of two or three impetuous spirits and steadied the rash ones, so that after fifteen glorious minutes we were on good terms with the hounds, and on the best with each other and our horses, and I was able to see which hounds were cutting out the work.

Tom Telfer and Billy Kerr and two hard-riding farmers, brothers, on young horses, were prominent in front, and close in our wake thundered and crashed a score or more of the best and boldest of Border sportsmen. The pace was kept for another twenty minutes or so, over larger enclosures with fewer fences and an occasional gate to open, which was usually done by the brothers alternately; though Tom, and a hill-man on a grey pony, seemed to be going out of their way to jump stone walls.

There was no perceptible change of scent, though hounds were slightly more packed than at first, and were pointing towards a hill rising straight in front of us and standing outside the range of higher hills behind it. As they got on to the base of it, we could hear there were few, if any, silent throats among them, and we realised that they had been going faster than was apparent, and we felt we might have to take from our horses all that they had to give us.

I watched the pack swarming up the slope straight for the summit, too steep for horses to climb. Which way round? Will the fox sink the wind, or will he keep on up wind? Having had a good start, and having had time and opportunity to make his point, and not being unduly pressed, he will likely do the

K

latter. This was the answer to the question mentally put, and was acted upon. Six or eight of us turned round the right shoulder, while nearly all the rest of the field in sight swung to the left.

It was a period of great suspense that we went through, losing sight of the pack altogether for five or ten minutes at least, and it seemed twice as long and I was beginning to sicken when I saw, barely half a mile in front of us, some sheep on a hillside run together, and shortly afterwards hounds moving up wind right-handed and rather across us, not so packed as before, yet not strung out, and all hunting closely.

We were now completely in the hill country, with not a cover or earth for miles round, and as the cool air rushed into my lungs I could not resist the temptation to cheer on the hounds, an effort which was emulated by half-a-dozen of the leading riders.

The next obstacle, on a rather steep slope, was a wall which we jumped. Tom Telfer, first at it, had pushed off the cope with his foot without getting down. Then came another which was lower and on sound ground, and which we had without waste of time.

Here hounds checked for some minutes but cast themselves well forward, and hit it off just as we got up to them, and raced away, turning backwards and running very fast through a nick between two hills and out of sight again. Only those who have hunted in a hill country can realise how suddenly and completely hounds will disappear. Here were we not three hundred yards behind them when they went over the crest, and when we reached it, though

A RECORD DAY

we could see all round for two miles apparently, not a hound could we pick up; they seemed to have vanished out of sight and hearing into space. A shepherd on a hilltop above us with his cap on his stick gave us the direction, and we pushed on. Some grouse, coming down wind with the speed of an express train, confirmed the shepherd, and soon we saw far below us once more the flying pack, sweeping along like a flock of pigeons before a tempest.

The line was now more or less parallel to the outward one, and about three-quarters of a mile from that, and it was not without very hard riding that we got in touch with hounds, who had gone very fast away from us *over* the hill. By the time we got into enclosed country again our numbers were reduced, and horses had had nearly enough. The two young farmers who had consistently led most of the way were there, one with a lathered horse and a mud-stained back, and Billy Kerr had vanished altogether.

'Twas here that I saw the last of Tom Telfer for a while. With legs and arms working, he rode at an awkward double with a strong hedge on the farther side. His horse jumped on to the bank rather free, and got too close under the second fence, and though he made a big effort to clear it, he blundered through the top of it on to his nose, and Tom temporarily disappeared from the chase.

One of the brothers, in jumping a low drop wall into a plough, found his horse get his fore-legs so deep into the ground that he was unable to get them out in time before his hind-quarters followed, and he was pushed on to his head and balanced there for a while before rolling over and lying still as if dead. But man and horse were up and going later on. The Irish mare had chanced a piece of timber and rapped her shins badly, and needed some persuasion to keep going.

We had some very pretty hunting here; hounds were desperately keen and unmistakably near their fox, but scent was not so good, and one after another would carry it for a short while, then fall back and allow a slower hunter to take it on and follow the short turns the fox was making. It was an anxious time as they almost walked over a bare fallow and on to the public road but not across it. After a short cast round in front, one hound, old Welfare, feathered and spoke on the road going along for about a hundred yards, then through the hedge and up a ditch on the inside for a short distance till she too gave up. For five or ten minutes every hound tried his best, all being very busy moving round with nose on the ground and stern high, but to no purpose. The field kept coming up, and several dismounted, got down, and loosened the girths of their steaming horses, believing all was over.

We were on some flat haugh lands, close to the river bounding our country, which was in full flood, and I was about to try down the river bank, when I saw old Rambler deliberately walk into the stream and push off to swim across the torrent. He was carried down a long way, and had some difficulty in getting out. Barely waiting to shake himself dry, the true old fellow worked along for

He was pushed on to his head and balanced there.

a few yards, then his stern began to go till it fairly lashed his ribs, and he proclaimed his find with an electrifying roar. Never was a note of music sweeter or more welcome, never did a huntsman tingle more, never did hounds respond quicker as they dashed into the boiling stream. Immediately half-a-dozen eager souls had plunged in, with the water curling up to the saddle flaps, and were struggling across the swollen river. Fortunately the foothold was good, and all got across but one, who got mid-way over, when his faint-hearted horse turned and took him back, while right and left the remainder galloped for the bridges.

Hounds were taking the line steadily across the furrows of a ploughed field, not making fast progress, but all in it; then wavering on the next field, an old grass one, until half-way across, they ran on at an improved pace. The next fence stopped two of us, and the Irish mare blundered badly, and I made the unpleasant discovery that she had had enough. Tom Telfer appeared on a second horse, which seemed as much distressed as his first one, and pointed towards a gate at which stood a boy waving hurriedly and holding a fresh horse. Who should this turn out to be but Ben with my good old friend "Royal"—a friend indeed, cleverly arriving at the most opportune moment. I blessed the boy profusely, and scrambled up with a feeling of exultation as the gallant old horse stretched himself out and flicked over a couple of fences as if they were brush hurdles. Tom Telfer and another were scrambling through a rough hedge as the old fellow had it faultlessly higher up.

Getting alongside of hounds, I saw Rambler, Pirate, Marmion, Woodman, and Regent running mute and with their hackles up, and as they crashed through the next hedge and turned sharp at right angles down behind it, I viewed, to my intense delight, the fox a short way in front, going very slowly with trailing brush and humped-up back. Hounds, too, got a view of him, and what a thrill they gave one as they opened their throats and threw their tongues with all their might, as they hurled themselves at him and pulled him down in the open, as he wheeled round to face them.

"Whoo-oo-oo-oop. Worry-worry-worry—whoo-oop," from half-a-dozen excited throats. "Well done, hounds." "What a good do, Master, eh?" from Tom Telfer. "Leave it, hounds—dead, dead—leave it."

"Well done, lads." "One, two, three, five, seven a half, nine, ten a half, eleven, twelve a half, fifteen a half; only one hound short; what a fizzer, what a cracker!" "How the devils drove ahead when they turned in!" "See me take that toss in B.'s farm?" "Thought we were going to lose him at Eckford." "What a rare fine cast of Rambler's."

"Brush to Mrs. Edgerston, I s'pose; only girl up. Would like that fine sharp-pointed muzzle myself. Just give me a moment to whang off all the pads; there will be bids for every one of them, by gum. Now then, tear him and eat him, boys. Whoo-oop—whoop. Too-too-too-t-oo-too—whoo-oop. Here's Billy Kerr coming up, and without his hat too, by gum."

"How far did you say?"

"Don't know; but it's seven miles on the map,

I know, from where we turned in, and we had been going for forty-five minutes before that."

"Here comes the Provost. Must try him for a drink. He generally carries a big glass bottle. My throat's like a lime-kiln. Eh, Provost?"

"Let's have one more whoo-oo-oop!"

CHAPTER XV

BILLY'S AMBITION

*"Happy the man who with unrivalled speed
Can pass his fellows."*—SOMERVILE.

DURING the usual walk out with hounds one afternoon, in the declining days of the season, Billy remarked: "I suppose you have just about got up to the top hole of your ambition, Master?"

Joanna, appearing at the moment, asked, as she kept Lavender and Beeswing back with a dainty little riding-whip: "Which ambition, and how do you suppose?"

"Well, only his ordinary week-day desire, I mean, something quite likely to be gratified, not anything outside the possible. I guess what it is, and that now, at the end of a successful season, he has pretty well touched it."

"Perhaps," I put in; "and if you will tell me your ambition, Bill, I may make a small confession."

"Right; you go ahead first."

"I'll tell you one of his pet desires," said Joanna, continuing to ignore my presence. "He wishes to make a record in sport, but is not over-confident of accomplishing it."

"What sort of a record?"

Her ladyship's permission to me to speak for myself

BILLY'S AMBITION

being conveyed in a glance, I blurted out, "Well, I'd rather like to catch a fox, shoot a grouse, and land a salmon in one day on my own place."

"Ho! ho! not so terribly immodest, and tolerably certain as regards the first two; but the combination is rather hyperambitious and touches on the extremely doubtful," laughed Billy.

"But he *has* done the two once," said Joanna, with an amount of pride she rarely displayed in her partner, again going on as if he was not present; "and he had a try for the third, and came home very much elated about it, though it was unsuccessful."

"Well done, my own uncle," said Miss Flo, who had been an interested listener; "go on and win. I know which is the hardest feat of the three, and I'll tell you how I'll help you. On some selected October morning when you are cubbing, I shall get old Geordie Mathieson as gillie, and I shall thrash the water all day till I hook a fish. If I can't hook him legitimately, I shall rake and sniggle until I do get him, and we'll have him ready for you to land after you have killed your cub and shot your grouse."

"Capital!" exclaimed Billy, who had been gazing at her with rapt admiration during all the time the girl was speaking; "that would almost make a certainty of it; and I don't mind coming with you; but to 'mak siccar,' when we hook him we'll just land him, and then put a line through his gills and hitch him up to a tree till the great man comes to land him, eh?"

"And this is the hero who only last night disputed the sentiment that all was fair in love and sport, and held that all sport should be played square," said Joanna, raising her voice and throwing it over Billy's head.

"I think I'd as lief have old Geordie for a fisherman as any one else," Flo continued. "Now tell us your little ambition, Mr. Kerr, though I have a fair surmise of the direction in which it lies," she added, little dreaming how near the mark she had hit.

"Don't give me away, dear lady," Billy had whispered, on seeing a mischievous sparkle in the eyes of the Mistress of the Forest fox-hounds.

In a mood of confidence he had recently confided to that trustworthy person that his ambition was to win the girl he loved best, and added with a heartrending sigh, "and to prove worthy of her"; a declaration which caused his hearer to howl with laughter.

"Seriously, I'd like to have a mount in the Grand National; best of all to ride the winner; but of course that is beyond my loftiest dreams; so I'd be content to get the course and nearly win on an outside chance. I'd really like to be one of that band of brave gallant men who set their face to ride out over these big fences at that terrific pace, and never grumble if they are knocked out, and the greatest ambition of their life denied them."

To which speech we all replied with one voice and equal fervour that we hoped he might have the chance some day.

Joanna took an early opportunity in private to tell me that Miss Flo, then several years younger and a very engaging school-girl, had confessed to her that she had no desire or intention to marry till she had had a real good time; that her ambition was to make heaps of friends—men friends—then marry the man of her heart; and that her boy should grow into a M.F.H.—a consummation which all who knew her saw no reason for not being realised.

"Now, Mistress," said both the young people; but Joanna adhered to her already pronounced declaration that "wild horses wouldn't drag from her what was her ambition, or whether it had been attained."

As we turned hounds over to Tom and the boy, I asked my super whipper-in, "If, preparatory to the ride in the Grand National which he coveted, he would ride old 'Royal' in the 'point to point,'" adding, "and if you win, you may ride him in the 'open hunt' 'chase the following week." His look of gratitude, and the vigour with which he sucked his pipe, were answer enough without words spoken.

'Twas well that the remaining hunting days could be numbered by units, for two of my horses were straightway taken possession of by my self-appointed trainer, and with some occult design, a third, the "Pearl," was appropriated by old Batters, from whom nothing more could be extracted than that he was going to "wund her up ti opera pitch." This was a favourite expression of his. "I have an opera gawin' on in here," he had once mysteriously said, unlocking the door of a shed in the back-yard used as a sick-box, and disclosing the resigned face of old "Safety," trussed up with a twitch and a tight-bearing rein, her fore-legs immersed in a tub of cold water.

So I had to submit, and had only the old lady and the "Omega" mare for the closing days.

On the former, on the last day but one, during a long gallop which took us to the heart of the hill-country, I was completely out-paced, coming up at the end to find a stout hill fox had been pulled down half a mile short of a strong open earth, amid the unrestrained yells of Tom Telfer and a score of ardent followers of the over-the-Border hounds.

And on the last day the Omega mare cut herself in kicking back at a wall of sharp stones, this being the only blood obtained, as Bill, with unnecessary frequency and doubtful humour, kept reiterating to me and to himself.

This last day was featureless, a fox not being found till late on in the day, and scent being faint and catchy, till by a turn of good fortune old Regent worked out a stale line which led up to a kennel in a small patch of whins, close behind a lambing shed, and pushed up a fat old dog fox, which was killed after a short scurry. With a fine grey mask and handsome brush, we found he was almost toothless.

This made up to the average number of foxes killed in previous years, so the last day of all, and the very last day of all which we had been contemplating, were reluctantly abandoned, and the entire energies of the staff were turned upon the "winding up" of the three 'chasers.

Of course the jockeys had to be wound up also; and much strange and spasmodic training was entered upon, more heroic and jerky than judicious and methodical.

The method of "Royal's" rider was, as he expressed it, to do a bit of fastin' and wastin', and after he had starved himself to his satisfaction, he found he could ride five pounds under weight; so, going to the other extreme, he rapidly made it up, and three days before the races a mean between the two systems was adopted. A private trial at catch-weights was carried out with the secrecy of a conspiracy, and it was hinted that some touting had been perpetrated.

The momentous morning came, and men and horses were on the field of action, the locality of which had only been disclosed by advertisement the previous day. The heavy-weight race and a yeomanry race had been run, and sixteen of the twenty-two entered for the twelve-stone race were starters, and their jockeys were weighing out. To the great disappointment of every one, Tom Telfer was among those who had not put in an appearance, and we heard he was suffering from a bad chill likely to keep him in bed for some days. Billy, I knew, secretly feared him, but on the other hand had been counting on him as a pilot to show the way by "taking the nearest road," as he himself put it.

Of course, "Royal's" jockey came in for a fair share of scrutiny, and he was surrounded by a small ring of criticising spectators as he was hoisted into the saddle by old Batters. He had a few words with Miss Florence before leaving the paddock, when he said: "I hope you won't behave like Mrs. Freddy Browne. She tells me she has driven twenty-two miles to see the race, and dare not cast an eye over the country, for her man is riding, and she cannot suffer to look on, but will sit with her back to the fun all the time lest she should see 'dear Freddy fall.' And what do you think she added?" continued Billy. "She said she couldn't bear the excitement of seeing 'Freddy ride a close finish.' I bet he'll finish long before the turning flag."

It so turned out that the gallant Fred finished in the second field, for, losing a stirrup at the first fence, he pulled up and trotted on to the knoll amongst the onlookers.

"No fear, I'll look out for the white blaze and the bang tail popping over the last fence into the winning field at the top of the crowd," said Flo encouragingly.

"There won't be much of a crowd by that time, I suspect; the open ditch at the bottom will take toll of a few; but I'll do my best for the Hunt and for the stable."

"I'm sure you will. The best of luck to you."

I had been more or less neglected by the Oracle, who, having instructed me in a laconic fashion, "I wad advize ye ti mak the rinnin' an' never heed whether ye feenish or no'," left me to scramble up unaided, as if my winning, or even getting the course, were matters of extreme improbability, and went over to Maister Willyum. To him the Oracle's parting injunction had been, "Keep him gawin' on, an' for ony favour dinna loss sicht o' the leeders, an' aboot a mile frae hame set him awa for a' ye're worth."

As we moved away to the starting field a covered fly drove up at a fast trot, a limp figure tumbled out of it and dived into the weighing tent, where a steaming chestnut horse was standing, and two minutes later a thoroughly transformed and manifestly workmanlike pair—thorough-bred horse and finished horseman—cantered down to the assembled group of aspirants to fame, where the roll-call was in progress, and as the starter called it, a husky voice answered to the name of Tom Telfer.

Acting on Batters' advice to set the pace, I allowed the "Pearl" to sail away, which she did pretty near the head of affairs for two miles or so, and without misadventure, to the turning flag. About this time I saw a chestnut horse putting on the steam, and with a mighty spring out and a twist of his quarters fly a mean-looking hedge, and I realised that the big ditch was behind it. The "Pearl" went boldly at it, but did not jump out quite enough, and landed in it, but without coming down, though she remained there for some time before scrambling out, dwelling long enough for me to see three or four others have it. Billy was one who got over without mishap, then two got in and went down, before the "Pearl" started again. There was now a mile and a half or so of good grass country, with stiff but fair fences, during which we heard crashing behind us and saw two loose horses going off in different directions. Two diverging lines were now available, one slightly longer, taken to avoid some heavy ploughed land, between us and the end of the course. As the "Pearl" drew up to her stable companion, the latter's rider hissed, "By gad, old man, I believe we are alone. Jack Elliot's and Bobby St. Clair's horses are both off on a line of their own. Dick Waldie is out of it."

"Steady, Billy, I'm going to try and beat you," I shouted.

As we could hear the crowd cheering and see the flag floating in the winning field, I asked the mare to go, but she could not stay beside the old horse, and after pecking at the last fence she dropped behind, and I had the satisfaction of seeing Billy's humped shoulders and squared elbows ten lengths in front, as he sailed between the flags.

"Bravo, Master!" shouted John Elliot's younger brother. "Well done, the Forest Hunt!"

"One, two, three, hip, hooray!" screamed Florence.

"Why, who's three?" I gasped, looking back at the string of riders coming into view.

"You are."

"How's that? I know Billy has beat me; but——"

"Yes; but Tommy Telfer has been in for some time, and is now at the weighing tent!"

And sure enough when I got there I found him surrounded by a cheering cluster of admirers. He was holding in his hand two pounds of loose lead which, as he had not had time to put into his saddle-cloth, he had carried in his pocket throughout the race. The Clerk of the Scales was saying, "You want half a pound yet; but there is your breastplate and your bridle allowance. All right."

When they came to examine the bridle of Tom's reeking horse they found it all mud-plastered and scraped, with the bridoon bit loose below the chin like a curb chain and the browband over one ear, in fact just dropping off. When told of this, Tom said, "Of course that was at the drop into the plough behind Borthwick's farm; the beggar stood tail end upper-

She could not stay beside the old horse.

BILLY'S AMBITION

most for half a minute and then ploughed along for about a whole feering on his head, and dashed nearly rubbed the bridle off—I hadn't time to put it on right again."

Incredible it may seem that any one should take a fall within a mile of home and be able to land a winner by the length of a street—yet so it was; and feeling it was no disgrace to be beaten by such a marvellous horseman, I said: "Congratulations, Tom; but what a ghost you look. Come up to the waggonette and we'll christen the cup."

"All right, thanks; but I must dodge the doctor, and then leather away home and get into bed before the wife misses me. I passed her on the stair on my way out, and said I was going for an airing, and might not be back for lunch. See you at Kelso on Monday next."

"But, Tom," said Billy, "how did you come in from Borthwick's? You must have come fairly straight. I didn't think you'd have had these two hundred-acre ploughs?"

"No more I did; for I got a fine bit of going along the headriggs, which you two blind buffers did not see were not ploughed. When I last saw you, Master, you were sampling the ditch. What? Here comes the doctor, by gum, I'm off. See you at the 'Chases next week, eh?"

Billy won the open hunt 'chase the following week, or, as old Batters mercilessly put it, "The auld horse wan the race in spite o' Maister Willyum." As a matter of fact, he was nearly caught napping in the straight, after jumping the last fence with a lead of eight or ten lengths; and he was so fired by a

L

desire for further fame that he accepted an invitation to stay with friends in the end of the week for a two-day west country meeting, where he had the promise of one mount, with the prospect of more.

On the Saturday evening, on my return from town by the last train, a hieroglyphic scribble from Joanna was handed to me. It took some time to decipher, and made the startling announcement that the writer was "going right through at once to nurse"—a decision which was painfully explained by the accompanying telegram, which read, "Mr. Kerr has had a heavy fall; rather seriously crushed; everything is being done."

A sleepless night of great anxiety followed, and Sunday morning brought a telegram: "Still unconscious; come." Now, Joanna was not an alarmist, so it was with sore forebodings that I started for the twelve-mile drive necessary to get the only Sunday train at the main line station. Two hours of a slow train, then a long wait, and a distressful cross-country journey on a branch line, did not hearten one up. Sick with suspense and misery, I got to the end of the railway journey, obtaining some slight relief by finding a dog-cart waiting. This had been sent to meet a nurse who had come on by the same train.

From the driver, an eye-witness of, and only too willing to recount the grisly details, I obtained these particulars.

The course was rather hard, and the stewards had put down tanned bark on both sides of some of the fences, a proceeding of rather doubtful benefit, as it caused some of the horses to overjump the obstacle. Billy had ridden twice on the first day and had got the course. On the second day he had a mount in a three-mile selling steeplechase on the second favourite, and had been forcing the running, his horse jumping rather wildly. In the second round he was leading by six lengths, when the favourite came up alongside and challenged him. His horse rushed the open ditch fence and overjumped it. The narrator said, " I declare to guidness the mere stuid back toonty feet an' flang hersel' at the fence." She crashed into it, and turning over, hurled Billy with great force beyond it and fell on him, rolling over him.

The doctors were in attendance at once, and he was carried to a comfortable farmhouse close to the course.

On my arrival things looked pretty black. Joanna, with a scared face, was flitting about noiselessly, carrying out the surgeon's instructions as promptly as if she had anticipated them, and said authoritatively, "Before the nurse comes in you may come on your stocking-soles and look at him for a minute if you like."

The sight of poor Bill, breathing heavily, and with half-closed eyes that saw nothing, was most upsetting, and his restlessness was distressing.

Before Joanna went to take her turn at the night's watch, we passed a doleful hour together.

"Oh, the pity of it! the pity of it!" she moaned; "this can never be his doom, to be maimed for the rest of his life!" Then with a groan and half to herself: "Poor, poor Flo; who is to tell her, and how? You know she's off yachting with the Douglases, and may see it in the newspapers."

Sitting up till the small hours for a report of any change in his condition, all the bright days that Bill and I had had together ran in review through my mind, and I saw him always good-natured, always cheery, always unselfish; proud of any small achievement of our little pack and jealous of its good name; with a keen appreciation of all the wholesome and natural joys that rational sport brings, and a power of enjoyment, and a love of life, and a hold on it exhibited by few: while oftener than all the other pictures that passed, was the one of that glorious September morning when we killed our first fox, and rode home through the shimmering hills, and when the talk turned upon the risks of hunting and he had said, "Anything but that!"

The morning report was "No change," and the consulting surgeon had diagnosed concussion of the brain and of the spinal cord, with a fractured pelvis, and he nearly made us all break down by saying, "It won't be immediate."

On Monday afternoon I went home. The telegram of Wednesday morning said: "Conscious now, but not out of danger; asking for you." I went through late on Wednesday night and found him very low, very restless with his arms, but not able to move his legs, and I was not allowed to see him.

On Thursday, the local doctor, a hearty man and a thorough sportsman, declared his opinion that "with the help of your good lady's nursing and his own constitution and pluck, there is a faint chance of my pulling him through."

Next morning I was allowed to see him, but he only pressed my hand slightly, and his smile ended in a

BILLY'S AMBITION

deep-drawn sigh, as he closed his eyes. Two days later the evening report was " A good two hours' sleep, and wishes to see you." I sat up with him for a quarter of an hour, speaking what words I could to soothe him and cheer him, and on leaving said, " I'll come early to-morrow and sit with you for a long time." Glancing back before leaving the room, I saw a question in his eye, so, going back and bending over him, he whispered, " Do you mind—telling—me—what was—wrong—with that—brown filly—you—sold to—my brother—last year ?—It won't matter—now."

.   .   .   .

Nearly twelve months later, that is, in the first week of the following April, Tom Telfer was holding up the stiff body of a brushless and headless hill fox preparatory to tossing it to the clamouring hounds, when he said, " I wish Billy Kerr was here ; " and then, " By gum, here he comes, and his missus with him. Let's wait till they come up."

A radiant girl rode up in close attendance upon a man whose clothes hung loose on him, and they were received with undisguised joy.

" How are you, Billy, old man ? Mrs. Kerr, here's to you ; real glad to see you," came from all in the little group ; and from Tom Telfer, " Just nicked in in time to see them tear him and eat him. Well done, you ! "

After the hundred tatters of brown were disposed of, Billy said : " Right glad I am to be here, I can assure you all, and right glad to see the end of this good hunt. I shall now be able to say I have not missed the season. I did not see much of the hunt, Master, but I heard some of it. My word, what a power of good it does one to hear the full cry of a pack of fox-hounds running hard in chase of a sinking fox that they have fairly and squarely hunted and run down; and I declare I easily recognised old Regent's and Pirate's deep notes, with Woodman and Pilgrim chiming in, when the leaders had for a moment overrun it, and Vanity and Beeswing squeaking in the rear. 'Pon my word, it beats cathedral bells."

"Yes; doesn't it?" echoed Mrs. Bill.

"Did it beat the Wedding March as you led her out of church the other day, Billy, eh, by gum?" said Tom Telfer; to which the two had no reply other than to smile rapturously in each other's faces.

Then, as hounds moved off for the last draw of the season, I said, "Are you coming on, Billy?"

"No, sir, certainly not," spoke out Mrs. Kerr, with decision. "He has done quite enough for a first day out. You are coming home with me, goodman."

"All right, pet; but let's just go to the top of Windburgh hill to watch them drawing the Hass. I like looking on from a hilltop."

"Yes; it seems nearer heaven always, does it not?"

"I'm quite near when I'm here beside yourself, old girl; but all the same, we'll go and watch them from the hilltop."

www.ingramcontent.com/pod-product-compliance
Lightning Source LLC
Chambersburg PA
CBHW020411230426
43664CB00009B/1254